THE MUSIC OF SILENCE

THE
MUSIC
OF
SILENCE

A Memoir

Andrea Bocelli

HarperEntertainment

An Imprint of HarperCollins*Publishers*

Originally published by Arnoldo Mondadori Editore SpA as *La Musica del Silenzio*.
Published in Great Britain in 2000 by Virgin Publishing Ltd.
Translated from the Italian by Stanislao Pugliese.
Reprinted by arrangement with Virgin Publishing Ltd.

A hardcover edition of this book was published by HarperEntertainment,
an imprint of HarperCollins Publishers, in 2001.

HarperCollins books may be purchased for educational, business, or sales
promotional use. For information please write: Special Markets Department,
HarperCollins Publishers Inc., 10 East 53rd Street, New York, NY 10022.

First paperback edition published 2002.
Designed by C. Linda Dingler

The Library of Congress has catalogued the hardcover edition as follows:

Bocelli, Andrea.
[Musica del silenzio. English]
The music of silence: a memoir / Andrea Bocelli ;
[original translation by Stanislao Pugliese].
p. cm.
ISBN 0-06-621286-3
1. Blind musicians—Italy—Fiction. 2. Tenors (Singers)—Italy—Fiction. I. Title.

PQ4862.O3366 M8713 2001
853'.914—dc21
2001039189

ISBN 0-06-093698-3 (pbk.)

02 03 04 05 06 /RRD 10 9 8 7 6 5 4 3 2 1

FOREWORD

I FEEL SLIGHTLY EMBARRASSED by the idea of attempting an autobiography at this point in my life, although I spent many pleasurable hours writing in my youth. Then, my writing was almost always confined to school assignments, but occasionally I sent letters to faraway friends, composed poems, or indulged in other similar adolescent endeavors. My intention now, if this can be a sufficient justification for a man of my age who suddenly decides to become a writer, is only that of passing some of my free time recounting the story of a very simple life.

My main worry is not that the reader might yawn over these poor scribbled pages or put the book down and go to sleep. Instead, it is that I seem to be observed by two eyes that read my thoughts while I write. They are the eyes of an old man with a kind face, a watchful expression, and the barely perceptible smile of one who knows the comedy of life so well that he now feels a sense of boredom and detachment. One cannot read the face of such an old man, whose passions are canceled forever by the inexorable forces of time, and the tenacious work of thought. And yet that serene face, illuminated still, perhaps, by the fire of ideas, seems to judge me severely. Beneath that gaze, I feel ridiculous, intimidated, incapable of anything, while a moment ago I was presumptuous and deluded, like students who believe themselves to be the custodians of absolute truths because of a few philosophical notions they have picked up in lectures. With the passing of time, I seem even to see a sense of irony emerging on the face of the old man. I ask myself then, why is he not indulgent with me, as he seems to be with everyone else? Why does he have to take *me* so seriously?

The reader, who perhaps has by now identified the inquisitor as myself as an old man, knows that his implacable gaze is always fixed upon me, at every moment of the day, and is at the root of my every act, my every decision.

INTRODUCTION

I AM IN ONE of my many cells: three yards square, two small couches, a sink, a small table, a closet against the wall. The small room is illuminated by a window that looks out onto the road. It is two in the afternoon and I have to stay here until the show begins. Soon they will call me for a rehearsal; later, for makeup; in the meantime someone will have brought me a cup of coffee. But for the moment I don't have anything to do.

I forgot: in the small room there is a computer. I think about how it might be able to help me to pass the time. I could write, maybe tell a story: my life, for example. But as soon as it forms, this thought fills me with embarrassment. I haven't written since I was a boy. Writing seemed a pleasant pastime to me then. Who knows what effect it would have on me today? I warn myself about being distracted from the performance I must give in a few hours. It's not easy, but one cannot live waiting to walk onstage. I get up and pace up and down the small room, in search of memories, nostalgia, people, distant images . . .

And unexpectedly a young boy in shorts comes to mind with nervous legs, a bit twisted, always covered in bruises and scabs, pitch-black hair, a face with regular features, and a knowing expression, unpleasant or pleasant according to one's point of view. I believe I can describe him as a normal young boy, or rather one with a common enough mixture of virtues and defects.

Normal in spite of a physical impairment, on which I must necessarily linger for a moment, if I want to speak of him.

Am I that young boy?

In some ways yes, but in others no, considering that I have changed so much since then. To speak of him as "me" somehow feels false, something I'd be embarrassed to do. I will pretend, therefore, that this book deals with someone else.

I will speak as though I am speaking of Amos. Amos is the name I have given him. I have also given him a family name: Bardi.

THE MUSIC OF SILENCE

I

EVEN NOW EDI, Amos's mother, never tires of recounting how her firstborn son grew up amid a thousand difficulties.

He was a lively, unmanageable child. "I would be distracted for an instant, and already he would have gotten into some trouble," she says; and if the questioner is disposed to listen to her, she will soon launch into an endless tale.

For example, she says: "He was never hungry. He was always that way, from the time I nursed him. Then, when he was a little bit bigger, I was forced to follow him around with soup plate in hand, to put a small spoonful of *minestra* in his mouth. I followed him everywhere: onto the tractors...the workers' motor scooters... everywhere." Or else: "One day I looked for him, but he wasn't around; I called him, but he didn't answer; I looked up and saw him standing on the windowsill of my bedroom, on the second floor. He wasn't even five years old."

And if the questioner shows no sign of impatience, she continues: "So that you can understand what I went through, I'll tell you this. One morning, in Turin, I was walking along a major downtown street, holding the baby by the hand. I stopped to look at a store window. When I turned around, only seconds later, I felt my heart flutter: Amos was gone. Desperately, I looked all around.

Nothing; he'd gone. I called him: nothing. At that point, I don't know why, I thought to look up and saw him up there, high up. He had climbed to the top of the stop sign."

As she says this, though, her expression becomes serious: "Amos was only a few months old when we became aware that he had a terrible pain in his eyes...blue eyes, very beautiful. The doctors diagnosed congenital bilateral glaucoma: a disease that sooner or later leads to complete blindness. From that moment on we raced from doctor to doctor, from specialist to specialist, from healer to healer...yes, we even tried healers, I am not ashamed to say. In the end our *Via Crucis*, our painful tribulation, landed us in Turin, where we went to consult Professor Gallenga, who was a famous doctor. We spent many weeks in his hospital. Amos was operated on many times, with the hope of saving at least some of his eyesight. We used to arrive exhausted from the trip, but above all prostrate from fear, from uncertainty, and bewildered by our own impotence. After accompanying us, my husband would leave and I would remain with Amos. The professor was understanding: he put a room with two beds at our disposal and we quickly became friends with the doctors and nurses, who proved to be indulgent in the face of Amos's restlessness. They even gave me permission to bring a little bicycle in, which Amos rode up and down the corridors. In this way he vented his frustration a bit. He suffered much, and it was difficult to calm him.

"One morning, though..." And while Amos's mother prepares herself to recount what happened that day, her expression becomes calmer. "Amos quieted down and stopped crying. We had just had an awful night and I felt tremendous relief at finally seeing him tranquil. I struggled to understand the reason for his sudden calmness, without success. All of a sudden I saw him turn on his side and press with his small hands against the wall alongside the bed. A little time passed, I forget how long, when I became aware of a silence that I had not noticed before. At that point Amos began crying again. What had happened? Why had that sudden silence upset him?

"And then, just as suddenly, he was calm again. As before, he returned to pressing against the wall near his bed. I strained my ears and became aware that music was filtering through from the next room. I carefully moved closer: it was a type of music that I did not recognize; probably symphonic or chamber music. It seemed to be the reason for Amos's tranquillity. I was happy because I had discovered something that gave him some relief from his pain. I went into the hall and knocked on the door of the next room. 'Come in!' I heard; the man who invited me to enter spoke with a foreign accent. I pushed open the door and saw him: he was relaxing in bed, two pillows arranged comfortably around his robust shoulders. He had the muscular arms and hands of a manual laborer. His face was smiling, open, but his eyes were bandaged. He was a Russian laborer; an accident on the job had deprived him of sight and he consoled himself with his little record player. I felt a lump in my throat, a deep emotion, and began to speak, to tell the story. I told him of Amos, of his reaction to the music, and asked his permission to bring my little boy to his room once in a while. He immediately said yes; even though I don't know how much he had understood of my account—he knew only a few words of Italian—the expression on his face suggested real joy at the thought of being useful, and a simple sense of solidarity . . ."

In this way, Amos's mother recounts how her son discovered music, whenever someone is disposed to listen to her.

2

THE DISCOVERY OF AMOS'S love of music triggered a cascade of gifts from his relatives, mainly related to the world of music. After a few music boxes able to reproduce simple little tunes, a beautiful record player finally arrived, accompanied by an LP. Amos was very curious about the record, but he wasn't really enthused about it. He preferred to listen to an old uncle of his who told stories about a legendary tenor who had recently died, Beniamino Gigli. After a while Amos wanted to hear the tenor's voice himself, and so, when the uncle gave him one of Gigli's records as a gift, the emotion he felt was such that he never tired of listening to it or asking his uncle questions. And Amos's uncle answered, at first drawing on his own memory, but then enriching his stories with anecdotes of his own invention or taken from the life stories of other singers. Many records would eventually prove necessary to satisfy Amos's curiosity.

Amos's uncle was a passionate fan of lyrical music and every once in a while let a new name fall into the discussion. Amos's imagination was quickly inflamed. It always seemed to him that whoever his uncle last mentioned must have been the best. His family quickly came to understand that records were the only gifts that made him truly happy.

From that moment the house resounded from morning to night with the voices of Giuseppe Di Stefano, Mario Del Monaco, Aureliano Pertile, and Ferruccio Tagliavini.

Then one day his uncle pronounced, in a special tone of voice, a name that Amos had never heard until then: that of Enrico Caruso. He spoke with vehemence and passion: he assured Amos that that singer had been the greatest, the most powerful, the most beloved by the connoisseurs.

After that, it wasn't long before the first record by Caruso entered the house, and that led to Amos's first disappointment: to the child, who was not aware how important the quality of a recording can be, the sound seemed to come from the bottom of a jar, that famous timber profoundly altered by the still-rudimentary instruments of recording. Amos thought the voice was not especially pleasing. Caruso, he thought, could not hold up in comparison with the noble and imperious tones of Del Monaco or the sweet and passionate voice of Beniamino Gigli, the voice that he had first loved . . .

Amos would come to change his mind about Enrico Caruso; but this happened much later.

⚜

One morning Amos was alone in the courtyard of the house, thinking to himself and walking back and forth, from the garage door to the gate that let out onto the local street. He was humming, as he did almost continuously, one of the arias that he knew. All of a sudden he heard a familiar step: that of Oriana, whom Amos called his *tata,* a girl who had seen him being born, who worked as a domestic in his house, and whom he loved a great deal. Oriana was returning from town, where she had gone to do a bit of shopping. While she opened the gate, slightly hindered by the packages she held, she saw Amos and called to him, waving the newspaper she had bought for his father.

"Listen carefully," she said to him, and showed him the big headline, which she read, carefully pronouncing each syllable: FRANCO CORELLI AMAZES AT LA SCALA OF MILAN.

Amos was eight years old and already knew about La Scala of Milan; but no one, not even his uncle, had spoken of that unfamiliar and—at least judging by what the newspaper said—famous singer.

"Who is Corelli, Tata?" asked Amos.

The good Tata began to read the article. It said that Corelli had displayed a powerful voice, very rich in harmonies—a true *"bronzo"*—and that the public had been enthralled by his high notes. Mixed in with the applause, recounted the journalist, there were cries of enthusiasm and requests for an encore.

When she had finished reading the article, Oriana remained for a moment with the newspaper in her hands, and to Amos she seemed absorbed in some secret thought. Closing the daily paper, she knelt down and whispered, "And he is also very handsome!" Then she added, "You must ask them to give you a record; I am curious to hear his voice . . ."

After a few days the first Corelli record appeared. It was Oriana herself who had found it and given it to Amos, asking him afterward, anxiously, what he thought.

Amos quickly ran to the old victrola, turned it on, set the turntable in motion, and lifted the needle arm toward the outside, delicately placing it on the new 45; and there was the orchestra playing the *recitativo dall'improvviso* of *Andrea Chénier* of Giordano. Then a voice insinuated itself between the pauses of the orchestra: *"Colpito qui m'avete . . ."*

It was a voice so different from all the others, ample and vibrant, swelling with emotion and an indefinable suffering; a voice that went directly to the heart. The singing was full-voiced, free, spontaneous, sweet in certain moments, strong in others, but always authoritative and true. A regal sound.

The *improvviso* is a marvelous excerpt, but it needs an interpreter able to really identify with Andrea Chénier, the great poet whose drama is rooted in the complex background of the French Revolution. The singing line must be elegant, convincing, and decisive at the same time.

The theme of the *Chénier* is intense love in all its meanings. When Corelli sang it, he seemed to have in mind the love for his art above all; that is, his love for singing. An art capable of inspiring, beguiling, and touching even those spirits most hardened by life.

Oriana and Amos, not knowing how to articulate these thoughts, were captivated by an emotion they'd never felt before, and the small boy saw Oriana cover her eyes while the tenor, with an incomparable sweetness, began the lines:

> *Oh giovinetta bella d'un poeta*
> *non disprezzate il detto:*
> *"Udite, non conoscete*
> *amor? Amor?"*

This last word was a cry of passion, a very high and noble cry. Its force, its beauty, left one breathless.

3

❧❧❧

THE CAR WAS READY; it was filled with everything necessary for the trip, and would shortly leave for Reggio Emilia. After
a thousand hesitations, which had cost Amos a year of school, a
boarding school had been chosen. The departure was sad but
necessary; it was a special school, in which blind and visually
impaired children learned to read Braille, studied geography on
relief maps, and had special facilities and equipment available. At
that time Amos was still able to see partially, but he needed to
learn Braille in case his sight failed, and to be with other children who faced the same difficulties.

As much as his parents forced themselves to cheer Amos up,
speaking of the new friends he would make, the games he would
play, and the things he would learn and then be able to teach his
little brother, during the trip the atmosphere remained heavy. His
father, Sandro, could not stand the idea of leaving his son two hundred miles from home. Amos's mother tried to give him courage:
she knew she had to act for the well-being of her son, and nothing
could prevent her from doing everything possible to allow Amos
to face life on an equal footing with others.

❧❧❧

When they arrived in front of the Instituto Giuseppe Garibaldi on the Via Mazzini, Mr. Bardi made his wife get out and parked the car; then he got out of the car, picked up Amos's suitcase, took him by the hand, and together they crossed the threshold of that dreary building.

The doorkeeper accompanied Amos to the cloakroom, where his suitcase was deposited, and then showed them both to the room where Amos was to sleep. It was a dormitory room containing ten beds, which to Mr. Bardi seemed too many; but then the doorkeeper showed them another dormitory room, where, dismayed, Mr. Bardi counted sixty-four iron beds and an equal number of night tables of the same material and color.

Children get used to everything, thought Mr. Bardi; but when he saw that in the bathroom there were only three toilets, in the Turkish style—three small, dirty, smelly stalls—and nearby a double row of sinks with a faucet only for cold water, he shuddered and felt his heart grow cold at the idea of returning home, to all his comfort, without his little one, who would remain in that horrible boarding school. He swallowed hard, to drive back the tears that rose in his eyes, and forced himself to follow along.

The doorkeeper introduced Mr. and Mrs. Bardi to a cleaning woman they met in the hallway and asked her to accompany them to the other places in the institution; then he excused himself, after expressing the hope of seeing little Amos perfectly integrated into the community.

The woman, whose name was Mrs. Etmea, guided the little group to a large room: "This is for recreation," she said, and Mr. and Mrs. Bardi glanced around the room, which was bare, though well lit by enormous rectangular windows. A piano stood against the wall; there was also a television and a small wooden stage.

"It's used for the children's performances and for the graduation exercises at the end of the year," explained Mrs. Etmea, before inviting them to follow her up a large staircase. Two flights up they found themselves in a long corridor; on each side there were many wooden doors, all the same, one after another.

"Those are the classrooms," said Mrs. Etmea, and added that there were others, even smaller. "One arrives from there," she said, and indicated a narrow staircase with a small door at the end that gave access to a small corridor.

She turned and descended to the ground floor, followed by the family, and invited them to visit the three courtyards of the institute.

The "small courtyard" was to the right of the main entrance. It was a space of only a few square yards, completely encircled by a wall and paved in cement, which seemed to be a perfect square. From there, many of the rooms on the upper floors received sun and air. On the other side, to the left, was the "middle courtyard." It resembled the small courtyard but was slightly bigger and graced by a portico held up by cement columns with square bases. "It's used during rainy days," said Mrs. Etmea.

From there a large, sturdy door opened onto a large piazza of beaten earth, divided into two almost equal parts by a line of plane trees, trees that in autumn (this was something that Amos discovered some weeks later) would cover the ground completely with dry leaves, noisy underfoot. It was the so-called large courtyard. Besides the larger dimensions, it had, compared with the others, a small boccie court.

That part of the boarding school raised the spirits of Mr. Bardi a little; he occasionally looked at his watch, shooting furtive glances at his wife.

It was late afternoon before the Bardi family left the boarding school. Amos's parents, who would remain in Reggio Emilia that night, did not want Amos to spend the night in the boarding school: they wished to remain with him awhile more, preparing him, and themselves, for the separation.

They ate in a small trattoria in the city center, then went to the Hotel La Storia. Amos slept between his parents, as he sometimes did at home: he still did not realize what was happening, or how much his life was going to change.

❧

The following morning Amos was accompanied to the institute. His mother entrusted him to a teacher, and promised that they would see each other at the end of the day. Amos was led into a room where several children were already seated.

He sat down as well and the teacher introduced him to his neighbor: his name was Davide Pisciotta, he came from Ravenna and was the eldest of eleven brothers. Soon after, Amos was given a piece of clay and asked to detach a piece and make a small stick. It was the first time that he had ever played with clay, and it was difficult for him to understand what he was supposed to do.

The room was a bit cold and the clay was difficult to shape at first. After a few minutes Amos understood the task but, intimidated by the teacher, who was watching him, did not stop until it seemed to him that he had completely finished his task. Even then, though, the teacher declared herself dissatisfied: the small stick was not smooth enough. A bit offended, Amos returned to his work in silence.

Every hour a bell rang. When the bell for noon sounded, the children were invited to rise and follow a new assistant, who led them to dinner. For Amos, the most difficult moment was fast approaching: that of separating from his parents.

He found them in the corridor that separated the room from the refectory, and he stopped, while the others, famished, continued.

Amos's parents gave him some advice before kissing him and telling him to go. While he was moving away from them, he broke out in tears. So his mother, after telling her husband to meet her at the car, followed Amos to the refectory, accompanied him to his place, and bid farewell to him there once again.

Amos grabbed her arm and squeezed it with all his strength. A strong hand seized him by the elbow and pulled him back. In the meantime, a voice was telling him something.

His mother's arm was slowly escaping. Amos managed to grasp a finger, but his sweaty hands could not hold on. For the first time in his life he felt alone amid so many people, abandoned to his fate. He despaired, shouted for his mother, but eventually he calmed down, sat back down, and listlessly swallowed a few spoonfuls of *minestra*.

When the *minestra* was finished, a waitress brought boiled meat with salad. Amos didn't like boiled meat. He raised his hand, as he was told to do in cases of emergency. Someone at his side lowered his hand and asked him what he needed. Amos timidly said, "I don't want this meat."

But the voice quickly replied, "You *will* want it, and you *will* eat it. Go on!"

In the meantime, with her heart in her throat, Amos's mother was saying good-bye to the assistants on that shift, who had accompanied her to the entrance door; then she ran to join her husband. He was waiting for her in the car, hidden behind an open newspaper: when she opened the door, she realized that he was sobbing desperately.

Mr. Bardi, who as a child had been to boarding school, had for some time harbored the idea of sparing his children that experience; but he was not able to do so. Amos's mother embraced him and sought to comfort him. Little by little, on the return trip, husband and wife began to feel less distraught. Thinking of Amos's future, they were sustained by timid hopes, by a fleeting optimism . . .

And then, there was their simple faith in having made the right decision for the future of their son.

4

THE FIRST OF OCTOBER of the next year Amos found himself seated at the desk next to Davide again. He was beginning the first grade.

The teacher was a woman of around forty who had renounced matrimony to dedicate herself completely to teaching and to her elderly mother. Miss Giamprini was respected as much for her capability as for her enthusiasm. Although deprived of sight, she had no problem controlling the class. Nothing escaped her. From eight in the morning, when the children entered the classroom, until the ringing of the last bell, she circulated among the desks, checking that everyone paid attention to the explanations; and if someone was distracted or placed their head on their desk or fell asleep, she knew immediately.

The study of Braille began with the consignment, to Amos and his friends, of a rectangular wooden case, filled with small *parallelepipedi,* also made of wood, that represented, according to their arrangement, the various letters; letters the students would later have to recognize by the very small points made by perforations in paper.

The teacher was indefatigable and transmitted energy and enthusiasm to her children. Often she organized competitions, which increased the commitment and general efficiency of the class; but she never forgot those who remained behind, and dedicated much time to them. Occasionally she worked the contests out in such a way that they could win a game, too.

Miss Giamprini possessed the gift of an unshakable and authentic faith, which to some made her seem bigoted. Every morning, before starting a lesson, she asked the students to recite a prayer, and she did the same before letting them go to lunch. Already she had begun to teach the children about the Bible, and such was the passion with which she told a story that the children listened to her with rapt attention, only occasionally interrupting her with questions or comments.

On the basis of that experience, Amos understood how an awareness of the Old Testament was of fundamental importance in the formation of children, independent of its strictly religious significance: an idea that later, as an adult, would continue to fascinate him. The Bible helps in understanding not only life, but one's fellow human beings and the history of peoples and their customs; one who knows it well is not astonished by anything and carries within himself an extraordinary force and security.

❧

That winter it was very cold and it often snowed. Amos went out into the courtyard with his companions and they entertained themselves by throwing snowballs. Perhaps for this reason he was often ill. He spent many days in the infirmary of the boarding school; there, Mrs. Eva (that was the name of the director of the infirmary) kept vigil over her little patients.

Amos enjoyed getting sick very much. It was wonderful playing or talking lazily with one's neighbor, far from the rigors and discipline of schoolwork. In the morning, very early, the nurse awoke and turned on a large radio that broadcast sweet and relaxing music. The children awoke, but remained toasty under the covers, awaiting their medicine. The food was better than what was served in the refectory, too, and the small patients were always sorry to be declared well and forced to return to the life of students.

In the spring, life at the boarding school became more enjoyable. The mild air permitted the children to stay outside a bit longer, and in the small courtyard one could organize great games of *legnetto*, a game that everyone was passionate about. The *legnetto,* made with tin cans or pieces of wood, was used as a ball. This modest object allowed Amos and his friends to pretend to be the world-class soccer players whose exploits they followed every Sunday afternoon, glued to their transistor radios.

Every once in a while the older ones showed off a *legnetto* that they had made themselves, a real luxury, constructed of an empty box of shoe polish, in which was a perfectly around piece of wood nailed to a T. The game of *legnetto* occupied a major part of the hours of recreation.

Occasionally Miss Giamprini organized a walk in the countryside. She was eager that her students not lose contact with nature. The countryside permitted her to explain things that in class would have seemed distant and abstract, and therefore difficult to understand. Almost always the destination of these walks was the house of a very dear friend of the teacher, a man called Orazio.

Because of an explosion and the fire that had followed it, Orazio's face was completely disfigured and he had even lost both hands; and yet, to those who met him, he was a picture of serenity, and even happiness. He was a pure and simple man, profoundly religious, and smiled often, happy to find himself among so many children and to display for them the "trick of the candle," with his head on the ground and his feet in the air.

There was something attractive yet awkward at the same time about him, an inexpressible irony in the face of life and small everyday problems, and a benevolent compassion toward his fellow human beings, even if the other person was more fortunate than he.

Before it was time to return to the boarding school in the late afternoon, Orazio's family insisted that the entire class come and sit in the small kitchen and refresh themselves with some home-made sweets and a drink. The snack ended with good-byes and the promise to return soon.

The next morning in school, Amos and his friends would talk at length of flowers and leaves, of animals and farming: Miss Giamprini made sure that those countryside experiences would not only be committed to memory but explained and fully understood.

❧

At the beginning of the spring the *maestra* announced that it was time to learn how to write properly.

One morning, in place of the wooden box, the children found on their desks a rectangular metal object, a metal rod, and an awl with a wooden handle.

Miss Giamprini showed them how to fix the sheet on the small table, and holding the awl high, she showed everyone the double line of small rectangular holes the awl produced, and explained that in each of those holes they could make up to six perforations. Then she asked that the class practice one in the first box, high on the right.

"This, children," she said, "is the letter *A*."

The children thus began writing, from right to left. Then, when they finished writing, they turned the page over and read their words left to right.

The time came to learn numbers as well, and the children were each given a small box of plastic material and a tin box that held a certain number of *cubaritmi*, little cubes on whose faces one could read numbers in relief, which in Braille consist of a number of signs followed by one of the first ten letters of the alphabet, starting with *A*, which indicates the number 1, until *J*, which corresponds to zero; plus a smooth face, which serves to indicate a comma and the decimals.

The four mathematical operations constituted a real stumbling block for little Amos. Addition in particular caused him great suffering: he could not grasp the concept of "carrying." It was easier for him to calculate the sum of two numbers mentally than to arrive at the solution by the method Miss Giamprini tried to teach. But eventually his mother removed the mysterious obstacle that was blocking Amos's learning.

He was in bed, convalescing after a terrible fever, and confessed to his mother his anxiety about returning to class. Again he would find himself struggling with problems that everyone except he himself knew how to solve.

Edi managed to perform a kind of miracle: after patient loving explanations and numerous examples. Amos suddenly understood. From that moment on and throughout elementary school, arithmetic became one of his favorite subjects.

5

❧❧

IN THE THIRD GRADE, Amos was interested in the first elements of geography and above all in history. His imagination raced frenetically. During recreation, he often played alone, and, walking up and down in the *salone* or one of the three courtyards, imagined himself to be a prehistoric man. He would have liked to live in a dwelling similar to the one he had made out of clay, under the precise and scrupulous directions of the *maestra*. Sometimes he imagined that he was driving a cart, identical to the one he had given to his parents at Easter holiday. He had made it himself, using a carton and some Styrofoam that he had carved and then covered with raffia palm. It was hard work and required much patience, and Amos was especially proud of it.

At the beginning of May, the children were given colored short-sleeved shirts and shorts. In the courtyards of the boarding school, under the gentle spring sun, they already seemed to breathe the air of vacation. The imminent arrival of their families made everyone happy. It was a happiness that infected even the teachers and assistants, who suddenly became more permissive.

Amos would soon again embrace his parents, his grandparents, and his little brother, and see his friends again; friends who would be able to fill him in on everything he'd missed. Not only that, but they would want to hear his tales, too, tales of a strange life in a world apart, very different from theirs. Perhaps only those who as children have been separated from their loved ones can understand the sweetness and profound joy Amos felt when he thought about the reunion.

May is a special month, above all in Italian boarding schools, where in the evening, thanks to the novenas and songs dedicated to the Madonna, the children can linger and enjoy half an hour more of play.

❦

Amos's voice had already been noticed by his friends and instructors at the school. If there was ever a solo part to sing, he was chosen to sing it. Amos did not hold back his voice even when he was singing in the choir: in fact, he was pleased to hear it emerge above the others. Someone thought of having him perform at the celebration at year's end, after the comedy performance of the older children.

Amos was to sing for the first time before the public. He was to sing unaccompanied by piano or any other instruments, alone on the stage in the recreation room, where for great occasions rows of folding chairs were lined up for the schoolchildren, instructors, assistants, and other staff: more than two hundred people in all.

The year-end celebration was the most eagerly anticipated and exciting day in the school calendar. The events began in the morning, with the awarding of prizes to the first in each class and to others who had distinguished themselves.

The dinner included a dessert—almost always chocolate pudding—and even a glass of wine. In the afternoon the preparations for the evening show began; the performance would be the climax of the day. Neither time nor labor was spared. The principal actors were chosen with care. To go onstage was an honor that all aspired to, even those who pretended not to care.

In the morning Amos had not received any prize and felt a

deep sense of humiliation. To appear as a singer was a risk, but also a vindication.

❧❦

The comedy that year was nothing special: it was a play concerning an unfortunate family with a drunkard father, a mother hopelessly trying to redeem him, and four children who were constantly bickering. The audience grew bored. At the end there was some chattering and little applause.

With the recital finished, it was the turn of Amos, who had been waiting in the wings for fifteen minutes, full of anxiety and emotion. He heard a voice calling for silence and an unseemly laugh that came from the hall; then his name was pronounced and a strong hand fell on his shoulders and pushed him, across a small opening, onto the stage.

The audience continued whispering.

Amos understood by that whispering that his performance meant little to anyone. If, from one point of view, the audience's lack of interest upset him, from another it gave him courage. He took a deep breath and began to sing, and his clear voice resounded in the room:

"Che bella cosa 'na iurnata e sole."

He had sung that first phrase all in one breath; when he breathed, he noticed, with surprise, that a great hush had fallen across the room. For a moment he thought he had forgotten the words. He breathed deeply and continued. When he reached the first high, *"ma n'atu sole,"* there was thunderous applause.

Amos felt himself reinvigorated. His heart, which until a few moments before was hammering with fear, now was swelling with joy. It was the first time in his life that he had been applauded.

Amos attacked the finale in full voice and sustained it with all his might, and the entire duration of his breath. Before fading away, his voice was overwhelmed by voices, cries, and hands clapping.

6

SUMMER THAT YEAR in Tuscany was very hot. Dripping with sweat, Amos and his friends played soccer in the courtyard and took turns refreshing themselves at a spigot on the corner of the Bardi house.

The play often generated quarrels, but the boys formed a common front, when necessary, against the exhortations and threats of Amos's grandmother Leda and Tata Oriana, who were worried about the health of the children and despaired over the fate of the flowers crushed by the football.

At the end of the game the children sat in the shade of the old arbor, from which hung fragrant clusters of grapes, and discussed the reasons for their victory or defeat.

One of those afternoons Amos began telling a story that immediately captured the attention of his friends. A few months before he had met a beautiful girl at his boarding school, there to visit her brother Guido. Her name was Elenora, and she was very well liked by everyone in the school.

"She spoke to a few people," recounted Amos, "but I realized that she always ended up near me. Suddenly I began humming something and she came to listen to me. We were together all afternoon, talking about ourselves, our families, things that we liked and disliked. She was very shy, but I encouraged her ..."

Amos was so caught up in his story that he didn't even notice that he had embroidered slightly the description of his first infatuation. Elenora, Guido's sister, really had gone to the boarding school to visit her brother, and she really did attract the attention of all the students—Amos in particular—but, partly because of shyness, and partly because her attention was focused on the older students, she had seen Amos only once, when he had hummed a tune so that she would notice him.

Amos had long fantasized about her; he had dreamed of wooing her away from her friends, of taking her by the hand and winning her heart; but nothing of the kind had happened. Amos, though, liked to believe that his dreams came true, and liked to make his little brother and his friends believe in his dreams. And so no one interrupted him, no one asked him questions: the subject was new to them all, and a bit mysterious. This did not prevent everyone from imagining a kind face, blue eyes, and a sweet and sympathetic smile.

Little by little, as Amos's tale proceeded, rich in details for the most part invented, those images became ever more precise. All the boys wished to meet Elenora; all thought that they would have been kind, courageous, and sincere with her. They imagined courting her, which consists of showing off one's best and carefully hiding one's defects.

At home, meanwhile, fervent preparations were under way for the meal celebrating the end of the harvest. The men would arrive around eight in the evening, with Mr. Bardi; they had cut the grain, harvested it into sheaves, and then thrown sheaf after sheaf into the mouth of an enormous threshing machine designed to separate the grain from the chaff; from another opening, on the side, not far from the ground, the seed emerged in robust bails that were then transported to the granary or directly to the mill. Even Amos had participated a few times in that work, in shorts and a short-sleeved shirt, an outfit that resulted in terrible attacks of itching, caused by sweat, dust, and insects.

That evening at dinner there would be discussion of the harvest, loud talking, joking, laughter, and Amos would probably have to sing something; it was the price he had to pay for not being sent to bed too early. They would dine outside under the arbor, and perhaps his parents would give him a glass of wine to drink.

This is what Amos was thinking about as he told his tale. Meanwhile he heard the women in the house discussing the seating arrangements and the quantity of the food.

Even that night the small singer was the center of attention. Everyone had something to ask him, to tell him, to remind him of; attached as they are to their own origins and land, country people are easily softened by the thought of a child forced to live far from home for a good part of the year.

Toward the end of the meal someone remembered Alcide, Amos's grandfather, who had died the preceding November. It was the first harvest without him. Leda was profoundly moved, and even her son had glistening eyes, but it was only a brief moment of sadness; tactfully Eda changed the subject, and all agreed that, at least for that evening, the book of the past would be closed.

When Amos went to bed he never imagined that a great surprise awaited him the next morning. Grandfather Alcide had died some seven months before, at dawn on November 4, 1966, precisely when the overflowing river Arno was spreading disastrously along the streets of Florence and elsewhere.

A few days before he died, he had had his grandson come from boarding school to see him one last time, and during his visit, he had promised to give him a horse as a present to take on trips into the countryside.

His father, who was present, had sworn to himself that he would fulfill that promise. So, a few days before Amos returned from boarding school for summer vacation, he had gone to Miemo, a town in the hills and forest not far from Lajatico. There, on the land of Mr. Baldacci, where the guards still performed their service on horseback, he had selected a beautiful filly, a small buggy, and a saddle. One of the guards led the animal to the Bardi farm and Sandro had immediately prepared a stall, begging everyone to keep the thing a secret.

Amos was still in a deep sleep when he heard his father calling him. Surprised at being woken so early, he dressed in a hurry, had breakfast, and left with his father to go to their farm: Il Poggioncino (the Little Hillock).

There was no one at Poggioncino that morning, except for Amos's maternal grandfather, Ilo, who was waiting for them behind the old manor house. The ancestors of the Bardi family had first lived in that house two centuries earlier. They had bought it with their savings after leaving their place as sharecroppers on the farm of the Corsini princes.

Amos threw himself around the neck of the old man and kissed him. He was happy to see him and had great affection for his grandfather Ilo, which Ilo only increased with tales of war, racehorses, dogs, cars, and hunting: all subjects that excited the imagination of his grandson. One day, they would talk about politics and women, but that would not be for many years.

Between his grandfather and father, Amos moved toward the corner of the house, where a small stall had been used for some time as a toolshed. He didn't know that his father had cleared everything out and had put the filly there.

Sandro stopped at the threshold together with his son. Meanwhile, the grandfather had entered the small stall. He emerged again leading the horse by the halter.

The child's surprise was enormous.

"This is Stella and she is yours," said the grandfather to Amos, who was staring at her dumbfounded. "She's good, you can pet her." Then he began with some advice: "Never go behind her, she might get scared and kick. You must always stay to the left of horses: like this, see?"

Stella had lowered her head and was grazing. The grandfather added, in a low voice, that this was the right horse for a child. The *avelígnese* breed, he explained, was made from crossing an Arab stallion with a female pony originally from the zone of Avelengo. That crossbreeding produced a small horse, very strong and able to adapt to any climatic conditions and, most important, of docile character. It was grandfather Ilo who had advised Amos's father, and he was proud to have contributed to the choice.

Soon Beppe arrived, the worker who lived at Poggioncino, and everyone gathered around Stella, who was first carefully groomed and then attached to the buggy. The harness was in perfect order. After examining it, Ilo adapted it to the size of the animal, who let him do everything, contenting herself by occasionally nibbling a bit of grass.

When the horse was ready, Ilo climbed aboard the buggy, called Amos to sit beside him, and cracked the whip. Stella broke into a trot. The buggy made its way down the access road, then turned left and moved toward the small street that led to the road between Era and Sterza.

The workers and peasants in the fields, observing the scene with curiosity and enjoyment, saw two glowing faces: that of Ilo, who seemed to have forgotten every worry, and that of Amos, transfigured by the pleasure of the moment and his faith in a still-untouched future.

7

LIKE ALL THE GRANDFATHERS of this world, Ilo watched carefully over his grandchildren. He had seven, all beloved, and he was always at their service, whether as a driver, a companion for games, or an advising oracle.

For Amos, he had a real weak spot; Ilo loved opera and became very emotional when he heard his grandson sing.

Every time he was at Amos's house, he begged him to get up on the step of the fireplace, next to the kitchen window, and sing for him; Oriana helped him up, and in this way, Amos, interrupting his play, learned to accept and understand his grandfather's tastes. He often sang the celebrated aria *"Mamma, mamma, quel vino è generoso..."*

As Amos's performances became more secure and convincing, the requests multiplied and the crowds increased.

Often, at the end of a meal, with the family together and before going to bed, they would beg Amos to grant them a song. His performances delighted everyone: was there anywhere a sweeter or more relaxing way to close a day of work? Sometimes

Grandfather Ilo would bring with him some skeptical friends, who invariably returned home touched and convinced.

By now everyone in Lajatico had heard of the voice of the little Bardi kid. "On the one hand, nature has taken something from him; on the other, it has given him something else," they said; and some, shyly, asked him to sing in church, at the end of Mass or during wedding celebrations.

Thus it was that Amos debuted in church, singing Schubert's *Ave Maria* during Communion, before a young bride and groom, in a church crowded with guests.

At the end of that performance, certainly juvenile and immature, many of the congregation had tears in their eyes; what had moved them, above all, was the contrast between the natural gifts of the child and his anything-but-natural physical condition.

❧❧

Day after day, the idea that only his vocal talents could attract the attention and respect of others became more and more rooted in Amos's mind.

Singing became for him a destiny from which it was impossible to flee: it was by now a part of Amos, as much as his face, reflected in the mirror, or his shadow, seen on sunny days.

Children like to be seen and Amos was a child like any other. All in all, he was not reluctant to grant the requests and accept the flattery of friends and relatives. To show off and arouse admiration seemed to him a game among other games, perhaps more rewarding than the others. Meanwhile his parents had begun to discuss the idea of enrolling their son in music classes.

Amos liked this idea. Until that moment, at boarding school he had been forbidden to touch the beautiful pianos that his older companions played every afternoon. Only once had he been able, alone, secretly, and with great emotion, to enter the room where they were, raise the covers, and run his fingers along the keys for a few minutes.

With the end of summer and his return to school, Amos was surprised to be called, along with other friends, by Maestro Carlini, the piano teacher. After a brief introduction, the first music lesson began.

Amos and his friends quickly learned how to read, write, and sing the notes of the scale. Amos was rather bored but consoled himself with thoughts of when he would be able to sit at the piano and begin playing.

It happened after a few days. Amos was alone in the room with the maestro, Carlini, and he was asked to play the first five notes of the scale, from low to high and vice versa, with both hands. After some minutes, Amos's wrists hurt, but he persevered, fearful of angering the maestro, who in the meantime was writing something on his own, ignoring the student. Finally, the maestro granted him a pause, but Amos couldn't rest for more than two seconds, because he had to tackle a new exercise straightaway. Amos wanted to play in his own way, as he did at the church organ at the end of the Sunday Mass, but he knew it was forbidden, and therefore he meekly followed the instructions of the maestro. But he felt a certain excitement when, for the first time, he was able to play a little exercise from the Beyer method. He repeated it dozens of times, dreaming about the moment when he would play it for his parents, and who knows, maybe for his friends in Sterza, who had never seen a piano up close.

One morning, after recreation, at ten o'clock, Miss Giamprini got out a box full of cases. Each one of these cases contained a flute. The signorina gave the instruments to the students and showed them how to put the flutes together, before explaining the position of the hands. She advised Maestro Carlini's pupils to seek his help. She closed the lesson with the wish that they would all manage to play something: "To draw sounds from an instrument is pleasurable in and of itself," she said, "*and* it helps to keep you occupied!" She added that even with the flute one could fight idleness, "father of all vices."

After a few days Amos already knew how to play a few simple tunes, and his reputation for music at the institute thus grew. Amos kept the flute in the small drawer of a night table, and in the evening, after going to bed, he would take it out and examine it; he was sure he had not explored the full range of its possibilities. The instrument exerted an inexplicable fascination upon him, as if possessed by a magical property. In the silence of the dormitory he could not play, but he simulated some movements, opening and closing the holes, until sleep began to overwhelm him, forcing him to put it away.

Even before the he took up the flute, Amos was used to holding and caressing something before falling asleep. It seemed that the habit quieted him down and helped him to exorcise, at least partially, his loneliness for his distant family. The practice continued until, from certain older friends, he learned to fall asleep in other ways, a bit sinful to tell the truth, but pleasurable and mysterious at the same time; ways that opened the door to an unknown world.

At that time, though, Amos was having more and more trouble falling asleep. In the silence of the dormitory, he heard the whispering of submerged and indecipherable voices—voices that were without doubt confiding secrets, telling stories, confessing unconfessable thoughts—and an occasional muffled laugh. Sometimes the assistant on duty sneaked in. He sternly admonished the entire room to be still, and when he left, the most absolute silence reigned among the boys. During one of those nights, Amos came to learn from his bed neighbor—a boy named Ettore, who was a little older—that babies weren't brought by the stork, nor were they discovered in the cabbage patch, and not even, as Amos had heard from someone, did they come out spontaneously and without any preliminaries from the belly of the mother. Ettore explained to Amos, in great detail, the way in which children are conceived.

When Miss Giamprini, with her acute sense of what was right, intuited that her students were discussing certain topics in a malicious and vulgar manner, she decided to hold proper classes on sex education. Beginning with the Sixth Commandment, she broadened the discussion to purely scientific aspects; therefore, after referring briefly to sexual relations, she spoke of the encounter between the spermatozoon and the ovule, of the formation of the zygote, of chromosomes, of the infinite possible combinations between them, and she described the development of the fetus, capturing the interest of the students.

Several days of lessons were necessary before the signorina was convinced that she had done her duty as a Christian and decided to shelve the entire subject. For Amos, it was a real victory to catch his parents by surprise and bring them up to date with his complete knowledge of a subject about which his father and mother had always been evasive, imprecise, and even misguided.

Now he thought he knew everything they knew, and therefore it was proper that they should consider him a man and speak to him as a man. He had always wished to seem older than he was, to do what the adults did, and to listen to their discussions. Amos did not want to be treated as a child because he did not feel himself to be a child at all.

8

⚜

EVENTUALLY THE DAY came to say good-bye to the school, the *maestra,* the assistants, the discipline. Amos waited impatiently next to his bed, with his suitcase already packed, for a ringing bell and a shout—that of the doorkeeper—who at the top of his voice would yell: "Amos Bardi is wanted at the doorkeeper's post!" His heart beat strongly every time the bell rang, but he had to wait longer than he expected because his parents had been caught in a traffic jam on the highway between Florence and Bologna.

They arrived around dinnertime, but the child's impatience was stronger than his appetite. They therefore left immediately. Amos wanted to return in time to meet his friends, maybe take a bike ride, see Stella, and lead her out of the stall to graze. A forty-eight-hour day would have been necessary to tackle even half of the projects he had in mind!

At home he found only his grandparents and his little brother, who were awaiting him anxiously. All his other friends were in the fields, lending their parents a hand. Patience. He would have to see them tomorrow.

It is not possible to describe the state of mind of a child who has just returned from boarding school after months of absence. It is a sweet sensation, a honey that bees do not know how to make, an ineffable peace, a childlike gaiety, sufficient for one to forget the long distance, the many hours of deep melancholy, the rigors of school, the envy of friends, the incomprehension of teachers . . . The joy of a return is worth the price one pays at the moment of departure.

❧

That summer, too, was very hot. Amos could not wait for the family's departure for the beach. They would be guests of his father's aunt, Signora Eugenia, who had an apartment at the Lido of Camaiore. But that was in August and it was only June. For the moment it was necessary to arrange something in the countryside. One morning his friend Sergio, who lived not far away, came to visit and show him his latest creation: a new catapult, more powerful and accurate than all their previous creations. Sergio had discovered a forked branch, had stripped and polished it, sawed it to the proper length, then had gone in search of an inner tube, and with scissors had cut two long strips, each a little over a foot long, and fastened them to one end of the branch. From the other he attached a piece of oval-shaped leather in which he made two small lateral cuts. In those cuts he passed the strips of rubber that he then tied with a strong, thin thread. Finished with his work, he ran to his friend, who had returned only a few days before from school, and they took up positions in the middle of a circle traced in stone in the Bardi courtyard, and shot at two pine trees in the courtyard.

On the first of August, the Bardi family finally left for the beach. Aunt Eugenia's apartment was spacious, but it had to accommodate two families, and became very crowded. Amos was set up in the room with "Aunt" Vanda. She wasn't really his aunt, simply a cousin of his father, but he had been raised to call all adult relatives aunt or uncle. Amos dearly loved Aunt Vanda; she spoke to him at night before going to bed, satisfying his curiosity about the most bizarre things. Sometimes she spoke of animals; she described the terrible voracity of the piranha, the ferocity of the *murene,* and so on. Other times—Aunt Vanda taught literature in high school—she recounted for Amos a novella of Verga or recited a poem, explaining the meaning of any words that were still unfamiliar to her nephew.

Amos, who was to begin the fifth grade, asked her about the difficulty of the exams and the most common questions. With great patience, Aunt Vanda tried to satisfy his curiosity and at the same time educate him on a series of topics, for example insinuating into the discussions an awareness of logical analysis and an understanding of history. Amos loved life in the open, among his friends, more than studying; but even so he listened with fascination to Aunt Vanda, who sometimes spoke to him until late at night. In the end, sleep would conquer them both and their voices were replaced by the deep, dark soughing of the sea.

When he awoke in the morning, Amos was alone. His aunt had already left. Amos called his mother and asked that she bring him coffee, but she refused: she wanted her son to get up, and not be lazy.

After breakfast, Amos went out to the beach, to the Buoni Amici Beach Club, which he liked because of their equipment. Besides the seesaw, which all beach clubs had, they also had a trapeze and chimes. Amos liked to grab the rings and get in a vertical position, with his feet in the air and his head down below. Old Aunt Eugenia and the other relatives were afraid that he would hurt himself, and this excited Amos even more. Like most children his age, he was a real show-off.

Amos often went in search of Raffaello the lifeguard. Raffaello was one of his friends. Once, before giving him a large seashell, he put it to Amos's ear and said: "Hear that? It's the sound of the sea!" He had strong arms and the muscles of a weight lifter, which Amos liked to touch. Amos was very impressed with physical force. At times he dreamed of being a boxer; other times a wrestler or a black belt in karate. Raffaello was his favorite, the living symbol of vigor, courage, and virility.

It was Raffaello who had taught Amos how to swim the previous year. As arranged with Amos's father, he waited for him around seven in the morning on the beach. He was sitting in a rowboat, with the oars in the water, and as soon as Amos was in, he moved away from the shore, rowing vigorously. Amos's father watched from the shore. When Raffaello got to the buoys he came to a stop, put the oars down, and tied a rope to an oar lock. The other end of the rope was knotted around Amos's waist; then Raffaello invited the child to throw himself into the water. But Amos didn't have the courage. So Raffaello, after insisting fruitlessly, picked him up and threw him into the sea. Before his fear could turn to tears, Amos found Raffaello next to him in the water. Reassured, he tried to impose some order on his movements. Raffaello calmly advised him, and meanwhile Amos's father, satisfied, called an occasional encouraging word from shore. Amos had first learned to swim freestyle, then the backstroke. This had happened last year; Amos now wanted to perfect his swimming in order to win the swimming meet that he himself organized for children his own age at the Buoni Amici Beach Club. He didn't like losing. Every defeat was a humiliation that just made him lose sleep. So he continued to ask for advice from his swimming instructor.

His family's return was scheduled for August 18. Amos, all in all, did not mind returning home, where he was to find something new: in place of the old woodshed and the "dark room," a new corridor would lead to a studio.

The masons were well along in their work: the corridor was ready, and even the studio was already plastered and tiled.

A few days after the return, the new rooms were furnished. Amos loved to sit at the desk, surrounded by his books and his things. That studio inspired in him a desire he had never felt before: the desire to study.

❧❀❧

The departure for boarding school that fall was less sad than usual. This was the last departure for Reggio Emilia. Somehow or other, he knew next year things would be different; Amos hoped he would leave the institute and be closer to home; and not only that, but he would have greater freedom to move about as he pleased and more time at his disposal. With these hopes in his heart, he took leave of his parents and prepared himself to face the fifth grade and the exam that would conclude this part of his life.

9

❧❧

"*MIO DIO, MI PENTO . . .*"

In this way the new school year began for Amos and his friends. They recited the prayer all together, standing, with their hands clasped, everyone in his place. Miss Giamprini prayed with them, walking among the desks. Immediately afterward, there were greetings and hugs. There was a strange happiness in the air, veiled by summer memories and worries for the school year that had yet to begin.

As soon as they were all seated, the *maestra* again took up recounting and explaining some Bible stories. The children enjoyed listening to those lively and often terrible stories, and therefore they remained attentive and silent, occasionally asking a timid question.

That year, Miss Giamprini spoke at length about the life of Abraham and his son Isaac; she also spoke, but more concisely, about Ishmael, the firstborn son of Hagar, slave to Sarah, who could not bear children. The children daydreamed at length about the vicissitudes of Job, they loved Joseph, who had a life of tribulation and wondrous episodes, and memorized the names of the twelve tribes of Israel. They even challenged each other during recreation to remember episodes or names from the Old Testament. It was the last year that Miss Giamprini would teach that class, and perhaps for that reason, she gave her best. She even decided to teach her students a little algebra and logical analysis before the end of the year; and since she loved nature, she returned often to the subject of the photosynthesis of chlorophyll. She wanted the children to love plants and animals, and to have respect for life and an admiration for all that the good Lord had created. With their fingers on the relief maps, the children followed the explanations of the *maestra,* who, as she spoke, passed among the desks checking that everyone was paying attention to what she said, in order for them to have a precise idea about the formation of the earth. As in years past, she organized occasional trips to the countryside. She also organized a correspondence, by an exchange of tape recordings, between the class and some German families, who sent, in very uncertain Italian, tales of their daily life. The German children spoke of their school events and their games. For their part, Miss Giamprini's students taped stories and poems, and Amos taped some songs. And in this way, his voice traveled beyond Italy for the first time.

In the fifth grade, the children were permitted to prolong their last play period—in the evening—for an extra ten minutes. Amos and his friends began spending more time with students from the middle schools. From one of them Amos heard of a drink that for several hours conferred an extraordinary power to one's muscles. It was obtained by dissolving an aspirin in a glass of Coca-Cola. Having absorbed the information, Amos had only one problem: getting hold of the aspirin, even though he had no fever or other illness.

He gathered up his courage and walked into the infirmary, where, during the last few days, a young nurse had substituted for the regular school nurse, Miss Eva, who was sick. He declared that he had an awful headache and requested a thermometer. When he had it under his armpit, he waited for the girl to attend to other patients, grabbed the thermometer, and with two hands began to rub the point. He was careful not to overdo it, to avoid the risk of being discovered: if the temperature had not risen enough, he would have tried again the next day. His heart was beating strongly when the nurse returned. Examining the column of mercury, the girl said, "Yes, you have a slight temperature, nothing serious. Go to bed, keep warm, and tomorrow you'll be fine."

"But my head hurts," protested Amos. "At least give me an aspirin." After a moment's hesitation, the girl consented. She found the pill and gave it, together with a glass of water, to the child, who pretended to hesitate.

"Well, are you taking it or not?" said the girl. At that moment another child called to her from the next room.

The few seconds of her absence were enough for Amos to quickly put the pill in his pocket and gulp down the water. When the nurse returned he showed her his hands and the glass, both empty, then quickly left the infirmary and made his way to the soda machine, from which, with a hundred-lire coin, he bought a small bottle of Coca-Cola. After he had drunk it, Amos certainly felt that his head was spinning a bit. He ran quickly to tell his friends of his adventure, and thought he detected in them, besides a hefty dose of curiosity, new respect and admiration. Then he sought out Antonio, the older kid who had revealed to him the secret potion.

Antonio patted him on the back and said, "You were very brave, but don't do it too often: dissolved into Coca-Cola, salicylic acid, which we call aspirin, becomes a drug, and is very bad for you."

He had adopted a paternal attitude and Amos felt patronized and deceived; his stunt had brought absolutely no benefit to his muscles and may have been dangerous to his health. He said good-bye to Antonio and went to bed. There he soon found himself in a cold sweat; his heart was beating faster than usual, making him anxious and preventing him from sleeping.

In the morning, when he awoke, he was fine. He rose in haste, prepared himself for the day, and tried not to think of what had happened the previous evening. Amos was very careful about his body; he was fascinated with the strength of men and loved movement. In boarding school he felt somewhat like an animal in a cage. Perhaps for this reason he was enthusiastic about an announcement of the imminent start of an Olympiad organized specially for the children of the boarding school. There would be light athletics, gymnastics, and soccer games. Everyone was happy and couldn't wait for the big moment.

❧

The Olympiad began one splendid day in May, a day so beautiful that it immersed the Emilian countryside in an almost Tuscan light.

That Sunday morning all the boys and their assistants gathered in the great courtyard to attend the opening ceremony of the games. The director, Dr. Marcuccio, gave a speech declaring how pleased he was about the event: the values of sport, he said, were a fundamental part of the education of a young man; he advised everyone to be good sportsmen and departed wishing all a good time.

Amos participated in almost all the competitions and even won a medal, but he did not survive the preliminaries of the high jump and dropped out of the marathon, which was run along the perimeter of the courtyard.

The next Sunday was the soccer game. Amos was supposed to play in midfield, but because of a sudden injury to the goalkeeper, Amos took his place. The two teams were tied one-all when he was required to make a daring play against the opposing center forward, who at that very moment was taking a shot at goal.

Amos was hit by the ball in his right eye, the one that allowed him to see lights and colors. When he got up off the ground, he noticed that his eyesight was foggy and felt a sharp pain that forced him to leave the game and go to the infirmary, where he was given an eyewash. But after a few hours the pain and the redness began to worry the young nurse, who, consulting with the assistants, decided to phone Amos's parents.

❧❦

The next day, Amos's mother arrived on the first train and accompanied Amos to Dr. Bruno, at the hospital in Reggio. After a brief eye exam, Amos was made to lie down on a cot in the clinic.

The doctor explained to the mother that it was absolutely necessary to stop the hemorrhage caused by the impact of the ball. He gently reassured the child, passing a hand through his hair, then called a nurse. Together they placed several leeches between the eye and temple of the little patient. They hoped that by sucking the blood, the leeches would help to normalize the blood pressure within the eye.

Soon the leeches were enormously bloated and had to be replaced. Amos was itchy but felt no pain. His mother did not leave his side, forcing herself not to be horrified.

Taking his leave of them, the doctor said that it might be possible to save some eyesight, but he did not hide his doubts.

Amos returned to the institute wearing a bandage over his eye that prevented him from seeing. His new condition forced him to face the possibility that he might very well lose his sight altogether. He would have to prepare himself for this.

In the institute he would pass from the class that was composed of those with some vision to the class of those without. That thought disturbed him and made him ill. For the first time he considered the idea of complete blindness.

He mentioned his fear to a friend, and discovered that talking about it gave him courage. From that moment on he tried his best to get used to the idea, as one learns to live with sadness or pain.

❧❦

When the bandage was removed, Amos realized that his sight was almost completely gone. He was barely able to see the lightbulb of a lamp. He felt an unimaginable sense of loss and bewilderment, and for a while hoped desperately that all would return to normal, but it was a vain hope. One morning, raising his eyes to the sky, toward the sun, whose warmth he felt on his face, he realized that he could no longer see it. Fear and desperation gripped him, his eyes filled with tears, and between sobs he called for his mother.

She ran and embraced her son in an attempt to alleviate his anguish, but quickly she, too, burst into tears. Amos had never before known his mother to cry, and those tears touched him deeply. He wanted to do something, to console her, but even within her arms, he felt himself to be powerless and alone, horribly alone.

He was almost twelve years old, he had just finished elementary school, and soon he was to start summer vacation. What would he do at the beach? How could he play with his friends? And how would his friends behave toward him?

❦

At dinner that night, even though everyone tried to talk of other things, the atmosphere was oppressive. During the occasional silent moments, it seemed as though one could hear the flies flying.

After dinner Amos went to bed and his mother, who didn't want to leave him alone, followed him up and went to sleep next to him in his little brother's bed.

There was a question that Edi wanted to ask her son, but she was afraid to. She wanted to know if Amos saw only darkness. She could not stand the idea that after so many sacrifices, so many desperate struggles, and innumerable trips to Turin, her son would be condemned to complete blindness. She buried her face in the pillow and began to sob.

"Why are you crying, Mamma?" asked Amos.

His mother did not respond right away. She gathered her strength and quickly asked: "Do you see only darkness now?"

"No, Mamma."

"Then what do you see?"

"Everything and nothing," answered Amos.

He paused for a moment and then continued: "I see that which I want to see. I see my room, the cupboard, the beds, but I see them because I know they are there."

His mother didn't understand what he meant. Then she thought back to the first encounter with the director of her son's boarding school, Dr. Marcuccio, who was also blind from an accident. Dr. Marcuccio had explained that even darkness was a visual sensation, and therefore a prerogative of those who have the gift of sight. "The blind," he added, "cannot see darkness, just like the deaf cannot hear silence, which is an auditory sensation, the antithesis of sound. That's all."

Edi had not cared to delve into that difficult explanation: Amos could still see then, and in her heart she hoped that he would always be able to see. Now, however, that discussion came to mind, and comforted her somewhat.

As for the rest, she knew that the only thing to do was to look forward with hope and help her son as she had always done; now more than ever, she had to dedicate to him all her physical and intellectual strength; she had to help him and encourage him. Perhaps all was not lost.

Amos could not stand his mother's crying. She seemed almost another person. He got up from his bed and ran to the other room, where he found his father, lying down but without his usual newspaper. He lay next to him, embraced him, and after some time fell asleep.

I O

THE NEXT DAY, Amos remained in the house. In the evening, he unwillingly ate dinner and went straight to bed. He had done nothing in particular, yet he still felt tired. Tired of thinking. Tired of his gloomy sadness, of all the seemingly unsolvable problems on which he had reflected during the day. Tired of that artificial naturalness with which it seemed everyone was treating him. Tired even of the attention, the kindness, the tenderness. In the eyes of others he wished to be as he always had been; but first he had to convince *himself* that nothing had changed, and that nothing would change from now on.

That was a summer of memorable decisions and events. The next day, Amos's parents spoke to him about the possibility of transferring to the Cavazza Institute in Bologna. There he could study in a normal high school with students who were not blind, while making use of the educational support of specialized teachers; in addition, he could attend the conservatory, which had a special section for blind students.

Amos's parents, though, were not convinced themselves about

the suggestion. Student demonstrations the previous year had created problems in the school in Bologna where the Bardi family was thinking of sending Amos. Students had occupied school buildings and held violent demonstrations, and the director of the institute had been found dead one morning in his apartment. It seemed that he had hanged himself because he could not bear the pressure and tension created by the student movement.

But it was Amos's first opportunity since completely losing his sight to demonstrate to himself and to others how strong, courageous, and responsible he could be. He did not want to waste it. After a few days, he resolutely announced that he wished to move to Bologna. There he would be freer, he would learn to move about in a city without anyone's help; in short, he would begin a new life.

A feeling of adventure, of entering an unknown and perhaps dangerous world (at least according to his parents), ignited his imagination. A mysterious force slowly took the place of his fears, uncertainties, and shame. Something in him began to be born—or at least to reawaken.

With the end of the harvest, Mr. Bardi accepted an invitation from his brother-in-law and traveled with his family to the Lido di Camaiore once again. Amos was worried about his cousins' attitude toward him now that he was completely blind, but was amazed and heartened when they acted as though nothing had changed.

His three small cousins, especially the oldest, were likable and independent, vivacious, and generous. Amos liked to stay with them very much, especially in the evening, in the bedroom, where they whispered to each other before falling asleep.

One morning Uncle Franco came back from the beach discussing with his wife the possibility of asking Amos to participate in a competition for young singers that was to be held at the Café Margherita in Viareggio. Amos overheard his uncle excitedly say to his wife, "I will accompany him to the stage and will bring him back at the end. Imagine the people after they hear him sing!"

Uncle Franco had already learned about how to sign up, about the rules and many other things, so when his brother-in-law and sister returned, he recounted everything in detail to the whole family. Amos listened, preoccupied: Uncle Franco was speaking of the public, which would no doubt be quite large, and as far as the orchestra was concerned, it was to be directed by none other than Maestro Maraviglia, the conductor of Luciano Taioli.

At five in the afternoon of a very hot August day, the young singer found himself before Maestro Maraviglia. If the audition went well, he would participate in a preliminary competition. If he won, then he would participate in the final competition, scheduled for the end of the month.

"What would you like to sing?" asked the musician, a bit surprised to see such a young hopeful. Amos replied that he knew only "O Sole Mio" and "O Campagnola Bella" in their entirety (the latter a song that his grandfather loved a great deal and often asked him to sing). Amos had never sung with an orchestra and on his first few attempts had some trouble understanding when to begin; he also had difficulty adapting to the tempo of the maestro; but after half an hour, he was dismissed with an invitation to appear the next evening.

❧

As he walked to the Café Margherita, with his father's hand resting on his shoulder, Amos felt burdened with a responsibility that made him feel ill. He had cold hands but was sweating. Behind him came a procession made up of his mother and relatives, as excited as if they were about to watch a soccer game on television. Amos wanted to participate in the competition, but felt unprepared for the part. He clenched his fists, thinking that by now there was no escape: he had to sing and win so as not to delude himself and the others.

He sat at a table and awaited his turn.

Every customer was given a voting slip with the names of the participants, with each order. Meanwhile, Amos was engrossed in his thoughts. When he heard someone call his name at the microphone, he awoke, got up, and, accompanied by his uncle, who had anxiously awaited this moment, climbed onto the stage, brushing past musical instruments, microphone stands, music stands, and a great number of cables. On the stage a technician approached and adjusted something; then the orchestra began to play the introduction to "O Campagnola Bella."

Amos's voice, surprisingly like an adult tenor, robust and vibrant, amazed the public, which broke into an ovation after the first notes. Amos smiled, reassured, and began singing again with even more vigor, until the end, which he sang in full voice and sustained with all his breath. His thin legs, his slender little body, his thin neck were all in contrast with that voice: a contrast that provoked an almost hysterical reaction in the crowd. Applause and cries continued even when Amos was passing among the tables to return to his place.

He was bewildered but happy. The audience's reaction encouraged him. The affection that he felt around him made him proud and full of faith in the future.

At the end of the evening, examining the voting slips, Amos was proclaimed the winner and was given a silver *margherita*—the Italian word for "daisy"; more importantly, he was now able to participate in the final competition, scheduled for the last Saturday in August.

In the succeeding days, at the beach and at home, it was all anyone spoke of, recounting impressions and referring to judgments they heard at nearby tables. A new suit and shoes were bought for Amos and he had his hair cut.

Sure enough, the long-awaited Saturday arrived. His mother accompanied Amos to the afternoon rehearsals, and after they were finished, she wanted him to lie down and rest awhile. Then there was a quick and excited supper, after which everyone hurried to get ready, turning bedrooms and bathrooms topsy-turvy. Around 10 P.M., Amos and his father, with his hand on his son's shoulder as usual, were in front of the Café Margherita, amid a great crowd of bystanders, and those who had not found a place to sit.

When the owner of the café saw Amos, he went to greet him and led him to his reserved place. After about fifteen minutes, the first contestant walked onstage. He was a big blond kid about eighteen years old, rather easygoing, immediately liked by the girls. Then it was the turn of a little girl of thirteen or fourteen, very vivacious, her voice very melodic, sure of herself; she, too, was very pleasing to the crowd, who applauded her with affection. Amos was nervously awaiting his turn, going over the words to the song. That night he was going to sing "O Sole Mio," his strongest piece. He felt faint from emotion; besides, an annoying stiff neck prevented him from any sudden movement. He realized that his hands were cold and that his heart was beating faster than usual. His turn was fast approaching, and the idea of walking onstage and facing that competition really wasn't sitting well with him. He asked himself how he would handle the disappointment and the shame if he didn't win. He *had* to win at all costs, but for the moment he could do no more than hope.

He was absorbed in these thoughts when he heard someone pronounce his name at the microphone and felt the hand of his uncle, who took him by an arm. He passed among the tables, among people who applauded, and climbed the small stairs to the stage. When the orchestra began what is perhaps the most famous of songs, Amos breathed deeply, clenched his fists, and fighting with his heart that was beating hard enough to break his breath, began to sing in full voice. Everyone suddenly became silent and stopped what they were doing: those who were drinking put down their glasses, those who were enjoying an ice cream put down their spoons, even the waiters stopped for an instant and turned to see if such a voice was really coming from a child, if it really emanated from such a childish throat, from such a small chest... When Amos finished the first verse, he took another breath and with all the voice he had sang the high *"Ma n'atu sole"* and was submerged by a hurricane of cries and applause.

Amos was encouraged. He had the impression, once again, of possessing his own will, of having conquered his nerves. The singing became fuller. By now he had won over the crowd, which was applauding so much they almost drowned him out. When he reached the finale, he again clenched his fists, and with the veins in his neck feeling like they were about to burst, launched into a last cry of passion, of pride, of liberation, and perhaps even of anger. The audience was caught by surprise: a deafening roar exploded, similar to that which arises in soccer stadiums to greet a winning goal.

Amos thanked the crowd. He climbed down from the stage and found himself swept up in a crowd of people who were shaking his hand and congratulating him. Some women kissed him. For the young singer, their kisses on his cheeks, wet with sweat, or perhaps saliva or tears, were not pleasant. He wanted to dry his face with his hand but was embarrassed to do so. He tried to reach his table and finally succeeded. He embraced his parents, sat down, and thought, I made a good impression. Even if he had not won, his honor had been saved.

The competition went on for some hours and eventually it was time for the winner to be announced. The presenter, with paper in hand, approached the microphone and began to read the results. He calmly listed the winner of fifth place, then fourth. In third place was a girl from Siena, who had seemed very good to Amos. After naming the second-place winner, the presenter paused to whet the curiosity of those present, said something that had nothing to do with the competition, then finally relented and invited the little Bardi to join him onstage to receive the gold *margherita*.

A female assistant went to Amos, shook his hand, pinned the

small jewel to his jacket, smiled, and wished him great success with his singing.

❧⸎❧

And that's how Amos won his first competition. He had every right to feel proud of himself, but from that moment, unbeknownst to him, a number of dreams and illusions settled in his mind and began to gnaw at him like termites. Dreams and illusions that—together with other factors such as luck—would influence his future, and would direct him along an unexpected road. But that road was still a long way off.

I I

✤✤✤

ON THE FIRST OF OCTOBER that year, with his gold daisy, his memories and his dreams, Amos crossed the threshold of the Cavazza Institute of Bologna. His parents helped him hang up his clothes in the wardrobe next to his bed, in the dormitory room at the top of the stairs; then they descended to the ground floor and bid him farewell. It was time for lunch and Amos went to the refectory, where, to his great surprise, he found a quarter liter of wine next to his glass. He drank it all, even before finishing the *minestra*.

At the institute he was the youngest, and also the smallest; in his case an exception had been made because to enroll at the Cavazza Institute you had to be fourteen years old. Amos was thirteen.

The rules of the boarding school were explained to him and he was given suggestions and information. The next day he left the institute at 7:30 A.M. with two school friends who, like him, had moved from Reggio Emila to Bologna. Without anyone accompanying them, the three made their way toward the Via Castiglione, under the famed arcades of Bologna, toward the middle school: San Domenico in the Piazza Calderini.

Arguing about directions they read from a relief map of the city, they carefully crossed some narrow lanes, knocked over a *motorino* carelessly parked by students under the arcades of the technical and industrial institute, and finally reached the Via Farini, where they turned left. They walked for another two hundred yards and turned left yet again, finally finding themselves before the door of their new school.

There were already a few children waiting and many others who had arrived were scattered about. A caretaker met them and accompanied them to class.

For the first time Amos and his friends sat at desks in a normal school, together with children who had normal vision: this was the path that the Cavazza Institute had chosen, because of the demands of the pupils, committed to the Student Movement. There was resistance, above all from teaching and nonteaching faculties, who, with the closing of the boarding school, lost their jobs, but the will of the students, emerging from assemblies and study groups, was to encourage, starting with middle school, the integration of the blind into society, and to promote access to work which up to that time had been considered unsuitable.

In the end, the students finally won. All in all, the closing of the boarding school, in addition to the conservatory, represented both a savings and a simplified organization for the public administration.

In 1971, when Amos arrived in Bologna, the battle had already been won. For the past few years the students had been regularly enrolled in normal state schools and the citizens of Bologna had grown used to seeing the blind students of the Cavazza Institute wandering about the city; every once in a while they would kindly assist someone in crossing the street or stop cars so that a student could cross.

Amos and his friends often traveled about the city, pushing always farther as little by little they came to know it better. On Saturday afternoons they would return just in time for supper. As for Sunday, they often stayed out all day, taking a sandwich with them, or perhaps eating at a schoolmate's home. It was a very different way of living from the tranquil life at the boarding school of Reggio Emilia. There, everything was calculated and planned, and nothing happened out of the ordinary; at Cavazza in 1971, every day was unpredictable.

The students were deeply involved in the Student Movement, which fought to revolutionize the world of education, and not only that. After dinner Amos often attended long meetings and listened with fascination to speeches about people and concepts unknown to him. Sometimes, as he thought of his family and friends, it seemed he was dreaming, or living on another planet, with no ties to the world from which he had come; then he returned to his senses. And with all his strength he tried to adapt, integrate, and become involved: something that, all in all, was not too difficult.

At the beginning of December, such extraordinary events occurred that they imprinted themselves indelibly on Amos's memory. Those events disturbed him, and caused many of his earliest certainties to crumble.

❖❖❖

Because of a disagreement with the board of directors of Cavazza—which, as usual, had no intention of conceding anything concerning the rules in the face of students' requests—the students' assemblies intensified, meeting even in the morning, during class hours. After three or four days, at the end of an interminable general assembly at which every student was present along with some others from the university, the decision was made around midnight to occupy the school for an undetermined amount of time. The staff was made to leave, and sentries were posted at every entrance door.

Full of excitement and admiration for the leaders of the movement, Amos passed his first sleepless night. He was assigned to be a sentry that guarded the back door which opened out onto the

courtyard. It was terribly cold and everyone tried to warm themselves as best as possible. The shift lasted an hour and a half, but to
Amos it seemed an eternity. When he returned, he met a student
from another school, who offered him a sip of grappa.

Amos didn't like grappa, to tell the truth, but partly because of
the cold, and partly to appear more adult than he was, he gulped
some down; after this he joined his comrades in the barracks and
with them began to dream about the possible developments of the
situation.

Around four in the morning someone got out a small tape
recorder and all together they listened to the songs of Fabrizio De
André, a singer Amos liked a great deal for his warm voice and
open-minded lyrics, sometimes bordering on the risqué.

The sit-in continued for three days. They were three days of
complete anarchy. Whoever wanted to sleep slept, whoever wanted
to go out went out, at whatever time of the day or night. Amos
went out to stock up on cigarettes, Tuscan cigars, and pipe tobacco.
Just as he didn't like grappa, so, too, he didn't like tobacco, but he
didn't want to seem different from the others; even if he didn't
inhale (inhaling made him cough), a cigar or cigarette between his
fingers made him feel more sure of himself. Sometimes he even
bought bottles of wine. Wine was something he really liked, and in
those days he drank more than he should have.

At the end of the sit-in, life returned to normal. The students
did not get everything they wanted, but the compromise that was
reached had persuaded them to suspend the agitation.

❧❦

The next Sunday, Mrs. Bardi came to visit her son and found him
changed: more detached than usual and less happy to see her. She
looked at him carefully and noticed that he had written something
on the palms and backs of his hands. She took his hand and read
some names: Karl Marx, Mao Tse-tung, Ho Chi Minh . . .

Slightly frightened, she asked her son for an explanation. With the serious air of adolescents who pretend they don't want to answer questions but in reality have a burning desire to display their thinking, Amos explained that in those first months in Bologna he had learned and understood certain things which until then had been carefully hidden from him.

"You and Father," he said, "or perhaps it is better to say 'we,' are bourgeois, rich people, or moderately rich, who live off the backs of the proletariat, exploit their labor, and travel around in cars with furs and jewels. I don't believe it's right."

His mother felt hurt, and reacted strongly: "You know I get up before your father's workers in the morning, I work more than they do, have more responsibilities and more worries; and we aren't as rich as you think; but above all, we have always worked honestly, your father and I, without stealing a lira from anybody. Don't forget that!"

Amos thought for a moment. His mother, he realized, was at least partially right. He himself had heard her rising early in the morning, he had seen her come home late at night, working whole days, worrying about everything and everyone. But then, where was the truth? Whom was he to believe?

For the first time in his life Amos felt the discomfort of someone who tries to believe in certainties but discovers that there are none . . . a tangle of thoughts, memories, sentiments, passions, and disordered concepts invaded his mind and he felt bewildered. Not finding a convincing way to respond to his mother, he let the subject drop.

They went to lunch in a small trattoria, then for a walk in the city center; but they were separated by a distance that had never existed before: something had broken the closeness they had grown accustomed to. In short, things didn't go well that day. Amos felt a certain mistrust of his family, but also a silent hatred for his school companions, who until then had only engendered confidence in him, drunk with the force of their ideas and their experience. He felt alone. Alone and uncertain.

*Andrea's parents on
their wedding day*

*Sandro and Edi
with Andrea a few
months old*

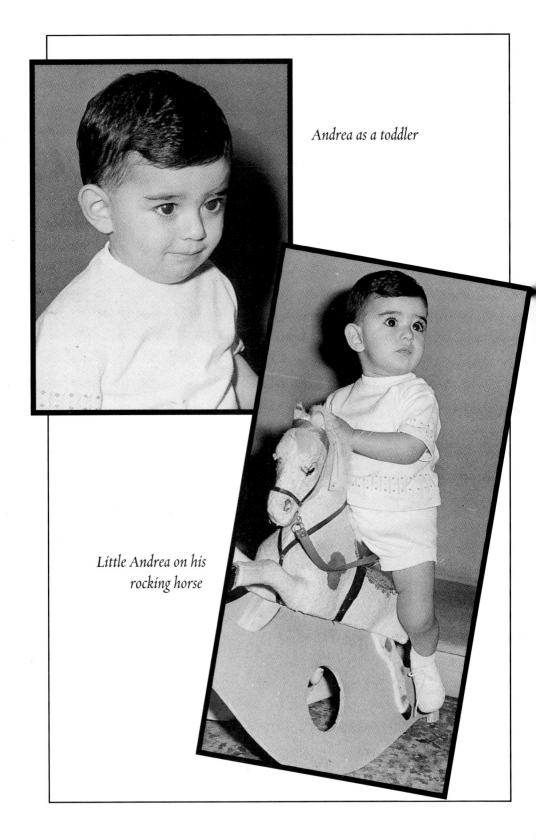

Andrea as a toddler

*Little Andrea on his
rocking horse*

Playing with a small
car for children

Young Andrea seated
on his parents' car

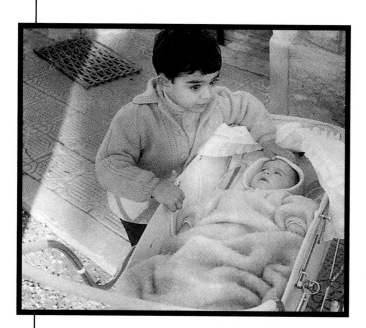

*Andrea with his
newborn brother
Alberto*

Andrea and Alberto

Young Andrea with Santa Claus

Andrea on a little tractor

Andrea riding his bike

Andrea and Alberto
at Viareggio

The boys on Sametto

Andrea on his first horse

Andrea wins the Margherita d'Oro (Gold Daisy) at Viareggio

Andrea and Adriano

*Andrea wins the
Frankfurt Festival*

All the Bocelli grandchildren with their grandfather

Sandro celebrates his seventieth birthday with Matteo, Andrea's younger son

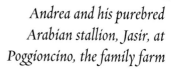

*Andrea and his purebred
Arabian stallion, Jasir, at
Poggioncino, the family farm*

Andrea riding Jasir

Andrea and his favorite horse, Jasir

Andrea with his Seeing Eye dog

Riding Jasir

UNIVERSITA' DEGLI STUDI DI PISA
DISCUSSIONE «TESI DI LAUREA»
FACOLTA' DI GIURISPRUDENZA: ANNO ACCADEMICO 84-85

Andrea on the day of his graduation

At one of his first concerts at San Remo, in 1991

Andrea in concert

Andrea and Alberto at Pisa airport, returning from a concert tour

Andrea and Alberto practice on the violin

Andrea with his fiancée, Enrica

Andrea at his wedding to Enrica

A birthday celebration

*Andrea with
Italian pop
superstar Zucchero
and his father*

In the succeeding days, the rift between Amos and his friends deepened, or at least so it seemed to Amos. The sense of fraternity that had made him bold was gone. It seemed to him that his heroes of a few days before were withdrawing and conniving behind his back, and that they guarded secrets which they intended to keep hidden from him. A deep, bitter melancholy possessed him.

One day, someone threw in his face the fact that he was bourgeois, a daddy's boy dressed as a worker. That evening, in the small room where Amos and his two classmates did their homework, a fight broke out that ended in blows.

When Amos felt the pain of a blow to the stomach, he bent forward, trying to breathe, then, with his head held low, he hurled himself with all his might against the boy closest to him, hitting him full in the face. The boy fell and Amos threw himself on him; meanwhile, a third boy pounded him with blows to his back.

With his teeth Amos grabbed an ear and bit it until he felt the nauseating taste of blood in his mouth. Only then did he let go. The fight lasted several minutes before someone entered the room and pulled them apart.

❧

The episode created an impossible gulf that increased Amos's solitude, his doubts, and his nostalgia for the familial, affectionate, and faithful world of Tuscany. A world that he felt would never betray him. He needed to confide in someone, but he didn't have the courage to do so. At night, before going to bed, he walked the halls of the institute, smoking one cigarette after another and counting the days until the end of the school year. It was not shaping up to be a good year: mathematics especially worried him. He had been falling behind and could not find the incentive to catch up. However things turned out, next year he would leave the school and enroll in a school in his province so as to remain at home with his family, as did most of the boys his age.

He had communicated his intentions to his parents by phone. They had listened without objecting, because what was happening at the school worried them more and more each day. But was Amos really ready to deal with a normal school, without a support network of instructors, readers, and facilities for the blind? The Bardi family feared they might be making a grave mistake. But Amos was implacable.

While the Bardi family pondered the problem of another school for their son, a new wave of student confrontations swept through Bologna, ending with a long and difficult occupation of the Cavazza Institute. Amos was present at the general assembly when it was unanimously decided to reoccupy the institute. Notwithstanding his recent second thoughts, he felt the excitement and enthusiasm of the first occupation during the new adventure. But isn't this almost always the case with adolescents when they are involved in situations that are risky and new?

At one in the morning the staff was driven out of the school and a sentry was posted at every door. Amos wandered up and down the halls, breathing deeply that air of disobedience and freedom. He held in his hands a pack of Nazionali without filters that he lit continuously and didn't put out until they had burned his fingers. For two days he didn't go to school. Fighting for the freedom of the students galvanized him.

One of those nights, Amos was selected, together with five other boys, to guard the main entrance. They sat themselves at the doorkeeper's table and began talking in low voices. The board of directors had threatened police intervention if the occupation did not end quickly, and that day riot police had been seen in the vicinity. For this reason, the sentries were jumpy and did not feel like conjecturing about what would happen.

Around 10 P.M., the bell rang, and Amos opened the small window that the doorkeeper used at night to check outside, before opening the door. A voice said, "I am with the police. I have orders to end the sit-in within three hours."

"So what?" Amos boldly called out.

"So either end the sit-in or we will have no choice but to enter by force."

"I'll refer this to the others," responded Amos, and closed the small window.

One of the sentries jumped to his feet and ran to the central committee, which was meeting on the second floor, in the game room; the others remained motionless at their posts, awaiting instructions. Some of them wished that the guard would be changed, but Amos wanted to remain there, in the front line, at all costs.

After a few minutes the doorkeeper's intercom rang. One of the boys picked up the small receiver and placed it to his ear.

"Okay," he said after a moment, and hung up.

"The leader said not to open up for anyone," he explained to the others.

Very good, Amos thought to himself. "So there will be a fight soon," he said loudly, and sat in the doorkeeper's chair, in the place of the "comrade" who had answered the intercom. There was nothing to do but wait.

⚜

In the hours that followed, the police rang the bell four times, and every time demanded that the students suspend the sit-in. Around one in the morning, there was another ring. Piero, a member of the guard, yelled in a stentorian voice, "Again! Who is it?"

"Police," came the response.

"So what?" answered Piero.

"We have received orders to enter. Open up or we will be forced to break down the door."

There was a moment of silence.

Here we go, thought Amos excitedly. He grabbed the receiver with his left hand and with the other pressed all the buttons of the intercom; to all who answered he said, "Come down, the police have given us an ultimatum."

At that moment his adolescent heart beat only for the revolution. From the main staircase there came the sound of feet, and in a few seconds the leaders were in the front ranks, before the entrance to the school. Amos got up and went to their side.

The noise of voices, footsteps, and objects thrown or moved became louder. There was a thunderous crash against the main door that startled everyone; a moment of frozen immobility; then another blow, similar to the first, which echoed through the entire lobby of the school. Yells and curses began to be heard.

A third and decisive blow was enough to break down the door. Riot police entered, immediately coming up against the students. There were many university students present who were politically committed and who had come, because of party solidarity or solidarity with the movement, to lend a helping hand to the occupiers of the Cavazza Institute.

In the hubbub, little Amos found himself disoriented. He wanted to punch, bite, fight, and show all his courage and his valor; but against whom? He was not able to determine who were the aggressors in that confusion . . . and even if he could, realistically, what could he do against men twice his size and trained for conflict?

He was realizing this when a blow to the stomach, perhaps from a knee, took his breath away. He fell forward and received another blow to his back. He was overcome by shaking and a sense of impotence and fear that brought tears to his eyes. He gathered all his energy and tried to make his way through the ranks of his friends, to get out of the fight, but it wasn't easy.

In the middle of the general confusion he heard the voice of one of the student leaders, amplified by a megaphone: "Do not resist. Everyone go to the auditorium for a general assembly."

The noise died down in intensity and the students started to retreat and then ran to the stairs. Amos, with shaking legs and a growing pain in his back, reached the staircase tottering, grabbed the railing as a drowning man grabs a rope, and as rapidly as possible climbed to his room, found his bed, and collapsed. He was overcome with trembling. After a while he awoke, undressed, and buried himself under the covers, covering himself up to his nose. He fell asleep almost immediately, but his sleep wasn't tranquil; every time his agitated dreams made him toss in bed, he awoke with a shooting pain in his back.

When the bell rang in the morning, he decided to stay in bed all day, complaining of terrible pain. The assistant on duty made him lift his pajama top and confirmed that there was a considerable bruise on Amos's back. The nurse agreed that the child should remain in bed.

"A hematoma like that is bad; I would advise you not to sit against the back of a chair," said Nurse Dedonatis with a smile. Nurse Dedonatis liked Amos, and often spoke to him about lyric opera and singers. Calm by now, Amos began fantasizing about leaving the institute and enrolling in a school closer to home. With these thoughts, he fell asleep again.

He awoke in the late afternoon. He was very hungry and still had an awful pain in his back. With cautious movements he got up, placed his feet carefully on the ground, and slowly got dressed. Then he went down to the ground floor, where he realized that the institute had grown quiet. The adventure was over, but it had left some traces in him: a vague sense of oppression, disappointment, and resignation; a free-floating unhappiness that somehow, little by little, was transforming itself into something else. Amos felt like a convalescent who is slowly regaining strength. Optimism was reborn in his spirit, and by some strange alchemy, disappointment turned into joy. He imagined himself already at home, master, finally, of his life. It was in this state of mind that he received an unexpected visit from his father.

Sandro was returning from a business trip to the small town of Treviglio, where the tractor factory that he represented in the province had its main office. He had decided at the last minute to stop off and visit his son and see how things were going. He had a school employee call Amos and took him to a trattoria not far from the school. When they were seated, he answered Amos's many requests for news about friends and his little brother. Then he suddenly changed tone and said with a certain solemnity, "Did you know that the workers in the shop went on strike?"

"Why?" asked Amos.

"They demanded a big salary increase and a reduction in working hours. There was a very long meeting in my office. Mario, whom you know very well, speaking on behalf of everyone, called me an exploiter."

"And you couldn't give them a raise?"

"Not that big. We don't earn that much from the shop."

"So what then?" asked Amos impatiently.

"So then I proposed to everyone that we form a corporation. In this way no one will feel exploited. Working for themselves, everyone will give their upmost, to the advantage of all." He was silent, raised his glass, and drank a sip of Lambrusco.

"So what did they say?" Amos pressed him, suddenly desperate to know the outcome.

"So they thought about it for two days, they discussed it, argued, and then decided to do nothing!"

Surprised, Amos asked why.

"Perhaps so that they can continue working less than me, to risk less than me, and to complain more than me."

Mr. Bardi changed the subject, as if he didn't want to give too much importance to these words; but they had been impressed on Amos, changing his ideas as a hammer and chisel change the form of a stone with small, knowing blows.

Accompanying him back to school, Sandro noticed a new demeanor in his son. There was an understanding between the two of them that made both of them happy. In saying good-bye there was a sense of camaraderie between them that delighted the father and made the boy feel more mature. One might have said that their old relationship, based on paternal authority, had evaporated in the course of that meeting.

During the trip home, Mr. Bardi was assailed by worries. He thought about the risks attending the Cavazza Institute entailed for Amos, but also of the difficulties that would present themselves if he and his wife really decided to enroll Amos in a school close to home, without adequate facilities for the blind.

On the road back he ran into a thick fog, and the trip began to seem interminable to him. At the Altopascio tollbooth he mechanically handed over his ticket, paid, and again found himself in the fogs of Padule, as far as Bientina, where the visibility was better. At Pontedera, the fog dissipated altogether. That road, so familiar and dear to him, began to put him in a better mood, and that good mood turned to joy when at home he found that his wife was still awake, waiting for him, to hear his news about their child.

12

⚜

IT WAS NOW LATE SPRING. Mrs. Bardi would get up very early in the morning and go to the bedroom window, open it, and look out at the stalks of grain that were slowly growing in the field across the road. One morning her husband found her gazing out of the window and asked her what she was thinking. She was startled; moving away from the windowsill, she answered with a smile, "When those stalks of grain are ripe, Amos will return home for the harvest and we'll all be together again."

"I think he might have to repeat some subjects this year," replied Amos's father. Mrs. Bardi was thrown off balance for an instant, then said, "Nonetheless, no one is to touch that grain until Amos returns." And she smiled at her husband.

At that exact time, in Bologna, Amos was preparing for school. He was sleepy again, and would probably fall asleep in class with his head on the desk. The previous evening he had gone out after dinner to the Da Ciro Bar, had drunk a couple of glasses of wine, and bought a pack of cigarettes and a box of Tuscan cigars. Then he had returned to the dorm and listened, alone, to some music on his new cassette player.

Amos tried to imitate the behavior and the language of his friends, but the smoking, the alcohol, and the cursing were not sufficient to bring him closer to the group; in bed at night, he made the sign of the cross and asked God's forgiveness for his sins: he would behave better starting the next morning.

Amos felt very alone, but what was worse was his growing sense of insecurity. He was missing the certainties that help make the lives of some adolescents so simple. His life was complicated by the seeming contradictions, by ideas and concepts so different from each other that they couldn't be reconciled, or even, for that matter, entertained at the same time. He also felt an indefinable malaise, which he attributed to his need to return home, to his environment, to the bosom of his family. He was surrounded by companions who possessed, it seemed to him, an unshakable confidence and certainty, which was the source of their self-possession. But something seemed to force Amos to mistrust everything, to analyze everything. It was tiring and depressing, and went against his impulsive, teenage nature. Amos had not yet read Seneca, and therefore did not know that people had always "preferred to believe rather than judge" (*unusquisque mavult credere quam judicare*). Much later he would understand, reading that passage from *De Vita Beata,* that the suffering and unease of those days signaled the building of his character, the foundations upon which he would construct his life, and were the beginnings of the force of character that he would display in the trials that awaited him.

For the time being Amos counted down the days that remained until the end of the school year. His grades didn't concern him: he knew that he could not expect much. But he would pay for his negligence during the summer. Then everything would change.

❧❧❧

June arrived and with it came the end of school. Amos failed math. It was his first real scholastic failure, but his parents didn't cause a scene. Their first thought was for the repeat exams; they wanted

Amos to arrive prepared for them, and to face the next year without any major difficulties.

Mr. and Mrs. Bardi decided to find someone who would help Amos read and guide him through his studies. So one morning Mrs. Bardi arrived home with a young woman called Manola. She introduced her to Amos, explaining that Manola would remain at his side for the entire year. And starting that morning, they would begin a review of Amos's math.

Manola was a girl from town, kind, educated, and very determined; she had been to school in Florence and was close to graduating. They began work in the studio of the Bardi house.

Summer had already arrived and a breeze blew through the open windows; scents from the fields, of food, the songs of birds, the far-off noise of farm machines, and occasionally the voices of men working in the fields drifted into the house. Amos was often distracted by those noises, by that so-familiar atmosphere of home. Time passed quickly and pleasantly.

After two hours of studying, Amos would run outside to call his friends, jumping on his bicycle and pedaling along the dusty country paths, returning later dirty and sweaty. "What a mess you are," cried his grandmother. "You look like something the cat dragged in!" Amos didn't hear her. After breathing the smell of wet dust that arose from the *piazzale* where his father had just finished sprinkling water, he ran into the kitchen, where the women were preparing for dinner. He couldn't sit still for a minute and his grandparents were concerned for his health. "You'll get pneumonia, sweating like that—calm down. Look at your little brother, how good he is!"

The brother, whom his parents called *Pace Santa* (Holy Peace) to emphasize how different his character was from Amos's, was sitting quietly, bent over a notebook with a pencil and eraser. He had to be called many times to make him come to the dinner table. Alberto was naturally inclined to study, and his grades were excellent. For this, he was the family's pride and joy.

He was a silent and introverted child, meticulous to the point of being finicky; but he got along well with Amos, who was so different, so quick to debate and argue. Amos was called *Terremoto* (Earthquake) at home.

During supper, Alberto sat quietly and ate slowly. The food was always too hot for him. He was still finishing the first course when others were already done. After supper he often fell asleep in front of the television and Father would carry him to bed. Amos, on the other hand, never felt sleepy and always had to be made to go to bed, either by cajoling or threats.

❧

For the month of August the Bardi family went to the beach again. That year, for the first time, they lived in their own, newly bought apartment. Her voice trembling with emotion, Mrs. Bardi had told her son when he returned from school that the apartment had cost ten million lire: their entire savings. Sure of having made a good investment, she was delighted with the new apartment.

Amos had to study so as to pass the exams he'd retake in September, so a math professor waited for him on the beach every morning. Her name was Eugenia; she was single and lived with her sister, who had two children the same age as Amos and Alberto, and a husband who, Amos had been told, was a wonderful, kind man, of noble birth.

Soon Dr. Della Robbia substituted for his sister-in-law and, full of zeal, dedicated his free time to teaching Amos the rudiments of geometry and mathematics. When he noticed his pupil becoming tired, he stopped the lessons and taught chess instead. He had won the regional championships as a university student, and now transmitted that passion to Amos, who, day by day, made great strides. Dr. Della Robbia drew chessboards on the very fine sand of the beach, and Amos loved alternating school geometry with the geometries of that fascinating game.

Amos had unlimited admiration for his new tutor. He even forgave his somewhat exaggerated self-confidence, a trait typical of those for whom everything comes easily, and who become popular and admired without being aware of whether their success derives from luck or their own qualities. Amos listened enchanted: Dr. Della Robbia would always win debates, whatever the subject. The pupil tried to assimilate everything the maestro said, and above all tried to please him by appearing quick and intelligent. The doctor excelled even in physical activities: an excellent swimmer, he also knew martial arts, having studied them in his youth; his whole life seemed to illustrate the saying *mens sana in corpore sano*—a sound mind in a sound body—and his pupil's spirit of emulation, which grew day by day, made the lessons seem easy. Amos thought that if he did well in the exams, the doctor would like him more. So he studied hard.

When he returned from vacation, Amos had changed. There were now new words in his vocabulary, Latin expressions he did not always use properly, witticisms directed at those present or not, and an ostentatious sureness that on the one hand made him seem perhaps less likable, but on the other helped to make him feel so much more self-confident than he'd felt a few months earlier. Above all, he was prepared: he passed the exams brilliantly, to the joy of his family and the pride of Dr. Della Robbia. Accepting an invitation from the Bardi family, the doctor passed a brief vacation in the countryside with his sons, Gionata and Francesco Maria, and his wife, Giuseppina, who adored him as much now as she had during the idyllic time of their engagement.

The Della Robbia family arrived one Thursday evening, deposited their suitcases in their rooms, washed up, and came down for a rich supper to celebrate Amos's exam success and departure from boarding school. Mr. Bardi opened some of his finest bottles of wine and everyone sang its praises: the master of the house beamed with pride because he had always involved himself in the health of the vines and the winemaking. Even the children were given a few sips. By the end of the evening, they were all overjoyed, without a care in the world.

The next morning the children slept late. After lunch Dr. Della Robbia suggested a game of chess. The boards were set up on tables, the pieces arranged, and a small tournament began. When the tournament was over and the sun began to set, the children wanted to go to the farm and see Amos's horses. They walked along the steep path, which allowed them to avoid the local road.

At the top of the incline they saw Stella, tied to a stake, and Fulmine (Lightning), a beautiful little colt that had been born a few months ago. Amos was eager to show his friends his courage and ability. He approached the horse, took the rope, and with some effort untied it from the stake and turned to the children, who were watching him from a distance. Stella followed him obediently, occasionally stopping to graze. Behind her came the colt, drunk with all the space he had at his disposal. The children crossed the farm road and Stella walked with them, while the colt remained in the field, uncertain whether to follow his mother or to remain where he was; but he suddenly decided to follow. Just then a car appeared, traveling at great speed. It braked, but too late. Fulmine was hit and in the fall his rear leg remained under the wheel of the car.

As he struggled to get up, everyone realized that the leg was broken. To reset horses' bones is practically impossible. The fate of the colt was therefore sealed.

Crying, Amos ran with the others to call for help. His parents sent the children home. They called someone to come and get the animal and bring him to the slaughterhouse. A few hours later a gunshot ended Fulmine's brief life.

That night at supper, Amos continued to cry. His tears fell, seasoning the pasta. He was amazed at the general indifference to the loss; his colt was dead and everyone already seemed to have forgotten.

❦

A few days later, with his brother and a friend of his mother's, Amos went to the conservatory of Livorno to inquire about admission to study piano; his brother asked about studying the violin. Both had to take an aptitude test consisting of no fewer than six hundred and ten questions, far too many, Amos thought. Amos scored first in the rankings and Alberto did well, too, coming in ninth.

Soon Alberto began to study at the conservatory with his usual zeal and commitment; he was very proud of his new Chinese violin. But Amos found himself strangely uninterested, and not just because of the difficulties posed by the Braille method. It was a new school year, and Amos found his attention divided between the middle school of Pontedera and the conservatory at Livorno, where his mother took him and Alberto twice a week. Usually Amos practiced his scales in the car on the way to classes, watched by Alberto, who, unlike his brother, was always perfectly prepared.

13

❧·❧

AT THE NEW SCHOOL Amos found a very different atmosphere from the one he had left in Bologna. No one spoke of politics, of independence from parents, or of drugs; they only talked about sports, holidays, schoolwork, the teachers, the best way of avoiding tests, or how to play truant without getting caught. To Amos all this seemed childish and he found it difficult to fit in, despite the fact that the other kids quickly learned to like him.

Pontedera is known all over the world as the place where the company Piaggio makes its scooters. Amos attended high school, living for the first time at home with his family like all the other students; and even if he thought it was comical to leave home with a lunch box and some change for a hot chocolate, it didn't take him long to adapt and to set aside his memories of life in a boarding school, which had forced him to grow up before his time. Besides, he wanted to enjoy the simple things, things appropriate for his age.

The teachers quickly came to like him and tried hard to make him feel at home. The boy he sat with, who was at the top of the class, considered Amos to be almost like a new project: he guessed that they had entrusted Amos to him so as to help him, and he intended to scrupulously fulfill that important task, if only to prove to the teachers how capable he was. Amos and Pietro were practically always together, during recreation, during gymnastics or music or art class, where Amos worked in clay; when there was work in class, Pietro would compile a list of vocabulary words for Amos, but he never told him any answers to questions the teachers asked because he was afraid of getting caught.

Behind them sat two small, lively, and enterprising boys whom Amos immediately came to like and admire. One was called Raffaele and the other Eugenio. Eugenio, the more open-minded and extroverted, was especially dear to Amos, who was similar in character. Eugenio was always ready with a joke, and very mischievous, which amused Amos. He was also a formidable runner.

Amos quickly became completely at home at the school. After a while, when he was there, he felt as though he were with his family. Professor Caponi, who taught music, adored him and did everything he could to have Amos at his side, even stealing him away from other lessons. Eventually, he wrote a song for Amos to perform at the end-of-year celebration, organized by the principal. There, Amos stunned everyone with his singing of the aria of Radames from Verdi's *Aïda*. Naturally, Professor Caponi, who was so proud of his pupil and his performance that he was practically beside himself, accompanied Amos at the piano. At the end Amos was surrounded by an excited crowd of schoolmates; he felt many hands searching for his own, grabbing him by his shoulders, and pulling him by his jacket. Eugenio, at his side, took advantage of the situation and chatted up the prettiest girls.

A few days later school ended and Amos was promoted to the next class with flying colors. He even managed to do well in mathematics, thanks to the work he had done with Dr. Della Robbia the year before.

❧❧❧

The holiday that followed was unforgettable, not because of any exceptional events that occurred but because of the uneventful peace and tranquillity, something that for Amos had become a novelty.

His father had begun remodeling the house and building a small room for the boiler, a laundry, a basement, and a new studio for his son in the barn, where the farm machines were then kept. The studio was illuminated by a window that opened under the arbor; there were marvelous bunches of grapes that already in August emitted the sweetest smell; birds arrived in great numbers to feast on them; looking suspiciously at the open window, they would peck at a grape and fly away, singing.

Amos loved his new refuge. He would sit at the piano and play something; then stop to listen to the sounds that wafted in from the countryside. The voice of nature enraptured him so completely that even music sometimes annoyed him, and seemed to break the spell. In that room, which the shade of the arbor kept cool even during summer, Amos would spend the first hours of the afternoon, reading, playing, or listening to a record; since he was incapable of staying still when listening to music, he would listen walking back and forth with his hands behind his back. From time to time he would receive a visit from someone. Eugenio came more often than anyone else; he liked to go jogging in the semideserted byways of that beautiful and silent countryside. To tell the truth Amos did not really enjoy these laborious runs; Eugenio was an excellent runner, and they exhausted him. He preferred the time that they spent in his studio. Eugenio liked to read and he was happy to read aloud: short stories, poems, the life stories of famous people, and sometimes something more explicit, when Amos would close the door and Eugenio would lower his voice.

In August, they went once again to the beach, to the flat the Bardis had bought the previous year. It was on the top—the fourth—floor of a very new building, built only three hundred yards from the sea, in Secco (the name of the area that surrounded the Lido di Camaiore). The children as well as the parents had rooms with a terrace; there was also a dining room, a small kitchen, and a bathroom, luxuries that the Bardi family could never even have dreamed of until a few years before. Amos's father's business was doing extremely well, thanks both to the extraordinary economic development of those years and to the hard work of Mr. and Mrs. Bardi.

Amos's father was a prudent, shrewd, competent man who was respected by his clients and colleagues alike; his mother, a woman full of fighting spirit, had been blessed with great business sense, with a gregarious, outgoing nature. They worked together side by side from dawn to dusk, and in a few years had transformed the small machine shop of Grandfather Alcide into an important commercial enterprise, where it was possible to buy and repair any piece of agricultural equipment. Now they could allow themselves to spend almost the whole month of August in their own apartment by the sea, and relax and enjoy their children and family life.

Amos returned to playing chess. He was able to play continuously because many of the children around had been infected with the chess bug. After a few games, he would throw himself into the water with Dr. Della Robbia's children, and they would swim as far as the buoys. Returning, he would take a cold shower to wash the salt from his body. Day after day his strength and his physical vigor grew, and while this gave him more confidence, it also made him a bit of a narcissist. He needed to compete with himself and others, to take risks, even to risk his life, because only in this way did he feel that he accomplished something.

One afternoon he found the Della Robbia children on the beach. They, along with some other kids, were looking at the sea, which had been very rough for three days. The waves reached almost to the first row of umbrellas. Amos immediately wanted them all to throw themselves into the water and swim; the waves, he thought, would pass over them. After a moment's hesitation, the doctor's kids accepted the challenge. The others refused. The three children walked forward, and when the water reached their chests, they threw themselves in and began to swim with some difficulty. Soon Amos heard someone call out at the top of his voice: one of the brothers was in trouble. He was caught in a current, which was preventing him from returning to shore. Amos swam toward their voices, and when he reached them the hand of the smaller Della Robbia boy grabbed his shoulder. Amos was pulled underwater, but quickly reemerged. He tried with all his might to swim to shore, occasionally reaching down with his feet in the hope of finding sand. Nothing. His strength was fading, and he was overwhelmed with panic.

"Help!" a voice yelled.

Amos tried to calm himself, and stopped swimming, trying only to keep his head above water. He called to the older brother, who said that the lifeguard was putting the lifeboat into the sea. Amos was overwhelmed with fear and shame. He tried to swim with his last remaining strength. After only a few seconds he sought the sand with his feet, found it, drove his toes in, and brought himself upright. Tears rose in his eyes and he turned to find his friends. They, too, were now safe: the current had carried them in to shore. From that moment Amos had greater respect for the sea, and perhaps some seed of prudence was planted in his exuberant and proud character: a character that pushed him to show the world his own bravery and strength, and that made him at times both a show-off and a bit of a fool.

❧❦

Amos hated it when people worried about him or assumed a protective air, as some do with the weak: he could not stand being treated differently. He felt himself capable of doing everything that other boys his own age did, and claimed the right to be treated and judged by the same standards as everyone else. "Be careful there"; "That's too dangerous for you"; "Wait for me to help you":

such phrases filled him with fury and made tears rise in his eyes. In the face of such concern, he would completely lose any sense of danger, and throw himself into doing whatever he was being dissuaded from. For all these reasons, horses, the sea, bike riding, guns, all these things fascinated him; in short, everything that could prove to others that they did not need to worry about him.

Don't give charity to those who don't ask for it, Amos sometimes thought, and tackled every enterprise head-on, convinced that he had to be the best simply in order to be considered equal.

The desire to learn and to improve himself, and the success that followed his efforts, strengthened in Amos the idea that not everything difficult was harmful. After every obstacle he overcame, an ever-more-conscious optimism took hold of him.

Amos was more and more convinced that life was a mysterious and fascinating journey during which we encounter many ideas that inspire us; then those ideas get mixed up with one another and drown in the sea of experience; from that sea other ideas emerge on their own, and these ideas produce other experiences, and so on. Every year we are all different from the year before; every episode, even the smallest, contributes to changing us, and we become the sum of all our experiences and conscious acts.

Amos had left his years in boarding school behind. Since then, he had changed a great deal, even if nothing from that time had been lost; he had simply laid it aside, with the care of one who wishes to lose nothing, because everything, sooner or later, becomes useful.

14

❧❧

AMOS BEGAN HIS LAST YEAR of school knowing that at its end he would have to decide what direction his life would take. Some of his friends would begin work immediately, but the majority would go on to various other schools. Amos had solemnly vowed to quit the conservatory, but had promised his parents that he would continue to study music privately. The truth was that he could not accept that a blind person could not be a masseur, say, or a telephone operator, or even a musician. No! He wanted to prove that it was possible for a blind person to do anything he set his mind to.

He had been struck by a phrase that a friend who was learning English often repeated: "Where there's a will, there's a way." Amos thought that this English phrase was more precise and elegant than its Italian equivalent: *Volere è potere*. Nothing that he ardently desired seemed impossible, and if people judged that something was beyond his capabilities, he felt obliged to prove them wrong. He asked his father for a horse that was livelier and faster than Stella. After a thousand hesitations, he purchased a pitch-black, medium-sized mare with a white stripe on her forehead. Mr. Bardi would have been disappointed if Amos lost his enthusiasm for horses. After all, Grandfather Alcide's dying wish had been that Amos develop a passion for them.

Amos's father instructed Beppe, who cared for the animals on the farm, to be careful and prudent: "Never leave my son alone with this animal, and for the first few times hold the reins when he mounts." Then, as if to ward off misfortune, he added, "I wouldn't want there to be an accident."

The mare was named Andris, and Amos went to visit her every day. Although he feared her lively and headstrong spirit, he always approached her resolutely and, with the help of Beppe, mounted her.

But riding Andris, Amos discovered his limitations as a horseman. He could not manage to control her pace or steer her in the direction he desired. If he used his spurs, she responded with threatening tosses of her head and even kicks in the air. Frightened, he would grab her mane and try to calm her. Fortunately, she responded quickly and would slow down to graze on a tuft of grass at the edge of the road.

Day by day, Amos's rapport with Andris became increasingly important in his life. She helped him to mature, to feel secure and serene; she made him love the challenges and goals he set for himself. She influenced his character and personality in a very positive way. When he was horseback riding, Amos felt in touch with nature, and his love for the countryside grew and deepened. The far-off sounds of the farm machines in the fields, the singing of the birds, and the silence all around gave him a sense of peace and helped him forget his worries. This whole world seemed to have been created for him, to give him peace and joy. He breathed deeply, inhaling the perfume of aromatic grasses, ripening fruit, orchards, manure, must. Sounds and smells penetrated his very being and gave him a sense of intoxication, blessedness, and physical strength. The teenage boy felt grateful, although to whom he wasn't sure—although certainly to those who had given him life. He even went willingly to school, feeling at ease among students who were removed from the acrimony of politics or pseudo-politics. Amos was sincerely fond of his friends, who helped him in a natural and spontaneous manner.

The teachers, for their part, were proud of having a boy like Amos among their students, for this gave them the opportunity to experiment with new and exciting teaching techniques, which they could then discuss with colleagues, friends, and family. Besides the music teacher, who truly respected him (he had given Amos an A on his report card), the literature teacher showed a real fondness for him, perhaps because Amos had discovered a passion, rare in that school, for fiction and poetry. Mrs. Bonini, who taught French, often spoke about Amos to her friends; at first she had been worried about him, but then he displayed a definite talent for languages: "He has an extraordinary musical ear that allows him to learn the exact pronunciation," she would say.

Amos knew and loved some French operas, such as Gounod's *Faust* and Massenet's *Werther* and delighted in committing to memory such famous arias as *"Salut, demeure chaste et pure"* or *"Pourquoi me réveiller."*

When Mrs. Bonini spoke one day of the poet Andrea Chénier, Amos was excited, his imagination sparked by the memory of hearing Corelli sing Giordano's opera by that name. He wanted to learn the original texts of the poetry Chénier had written just before his death by guillotine, his own blood soaking the cuffs of his shirt. While the rest of the class yawned and waited for the bell to ring, Amos alone had memorized those verses, and when he went home for lunch, he recited them to his parents.

"Comme un dernier rayon, comme un dernier sourire animent la fin d'un beau jour, au pied de l'échafaud j'essaye encore ma lyre: peut-être est-ce bientôt mon tour?"

He paused briefly and then translated for those who had not understood. "As a last ray, as a last smile gives life to the end of a beautiful day, I write my poetry at the foot of the scaffold: perhaps it will soon be my turn." It seemed to him that his parents admired this little performance, without sharing the profound emotion. For he alone was able to trace those lines back to the notes of Giordano, the voice of Corelli, and the verses to the aria *"Come un bel dì di Maggio."* He felt he was immersed in a world all his own. He tried to imagine the era in which Chénier lived, an age in which people fought and killed one another with such ruthlessness. Amos wanted to learn more about the French Revolution, but his teachers offered only fragmentary and disconnected information; it seemed as though they were distracted and were answering his questions halfheartedly. Although he was disappointed, he stopped daydreaming and eventually regained a sense of reality. He returned to being a little rascal, the boy always ready for a joke or a laugh, "always up to something," as they said at home.

Meanwhile, exams were coming up. A good performance would allow Amos to enter the upper schools. He looked to the future with optimism and faith in himself, rather than in anyone else. Every morning, with his book bag slung over his shoulder and his typewriter in hand, he would approach the bus stop with his younger brother, Alberto, just like a brave, proud soldier full of great hopes.

He would climb on the bus and almost always sit in the back among the older boys. He listened silently to their discussions, feeling somewhat detached. Although Amos felt neither disdainful nor uninterested, he sensed that their feelings and their world were different from his. There was something that prevented the boy from fully sharing that other world, and he really had no desire to do so.

When he got off the bus in Pontedera, Amos walked quickly to the courtyard of the school, where many of his classmates had already assembled. To fight off the dampness of those winter mornings, he would sometimes play-fight briefly with someone. After a bit of physical activity, he was more inclined to sit down at a desk for five interminable hours.

At the sound of the last bell, which everyone waited for with keen anticipation, Amos was always among the first to reach the gates, together with Eugenio and another classmate, but there they had to stop and wait for a brother from one of the religious orders. He always arrived late, slow as he was, putting everything in order, paying his respects to the teachers, and finally opening the gates.

Amos's professors found his work more than respectable, and he approached the final exams calmly and was graduated with honors. Two of his friends (one was Eugenio) earned the distinction of "outstanding." Amos was among the top five in his class and was pleased, as were his mother and father.

It was time for the most important decision: Amos had to choose the direction his life would take, then seriously commit himself to it. A few days after the exams, his father entered his room and, finding him still in bed, sat down on a wooden chest and talked to him about his responsibilities. "It's time for you to make some choices; there's no time to lose. Think hard and make a definite decision; then you can enjoy your vacation," he said in a calm but resolute tone.

Amos knew he could choose the school he wanted to attend, but he also knew that he was expected to enroll in the secondary school and, after five years, receive a classical diploma. Everyone in the family felt that was the right direction for an intelligent boy who was inclined more toward literature than scientific subjects.

The more he thought about it the more willing Amos was to follow this advice. It seemed to be the right choice, and in any event, he had no intention of disappointing his parents. So he put aside any reservations and told his father that he would enroll in the classical lycée in Pontedera, where he would study Greek and Latin, at the cost of putting aside music, and would become "a man of letters," thus realizing his family's hopes for him.

Having cleared his mind of that worry, he devoted himself to planning his vacation, half of which he would spend in the countryside and half at the beach with his family, as they now did every year. The apartment at the beach, while not large, was cozy, comfortable, and intimate. After dinner, Amos loved to go out onto the balcony facing the sea and inhale the salty air. The rougher the sea, the more calm and tranquil he felt. But he wasn't entirely serene: for the previous few days, he had felt something in his veins, something that troubled his dreams at night as well as those daylight hours when he listened to music and paced up and down in his room. He walked, reflected, and dreamed, trying to understand what he was feeling. For several days, a pale, sweet face with regular features returned again and again to his thoughts. It was the face of a girl on the threshold of womanhood. She had long blond hair and blue eyes full of the joy of life.

Amos had met her at the beach. His friends spoke of nothing else and followed her everywhere, unable to take their eyes off her. He had idealized her, imagining her to be as beautiful inside as she was on the surface; an angel from heaven. From that angel, however, he received no sign. No particular attention, no act of kindness that would permit a hope to flower. True, she spoke to him in a respectful and polite tone, but perhaps she did this only to spare his feelings. At least that's what he thought. Alessandra had a boyfriend, so even his friends didn't get anywhere with her. Although Amos knew she was involved for the moment, he hoped one day that she and her boyfriend would break up. In the meantime, he thought about her constantly.

She was Amos's first love, and he felt he had to do something—something different from what the others were doing. And so, lying on his bed, his door locked, he attempted to compose verses to give her secretly: *"Oh, mia fanciulla dai capelli biondi / bocca ridente, e occhi giocondi..."* ("Oh, my young girl with blond hair / smiling mouth, and joyful eyes..."). He put together a dozen rhymed poems and then stopped and began to think of a way to give them to her. At first, he thought that the best thing to do would be to recite them to her personally, but then realized almost immediately that he could never do this. How would he feel if she began to laugh or, worse, made fun of him? No, it was better to give her the handwritten poems, Amos decided. But to whom would he dictate these poems? To whom could he confess the name of the intended recipient?

In the end Amos decided to do nothing: he would hold these poems in his heart, keep them a secret. Thinking that this was his first secret of an amorous nature, he felt the blood flow to his cheeks, so he got up off the bed and went to his tape player. Better to distract himself with some music, he thought. Then he pulled open the shutter onto the balcony and let in some air. As the spools of his old Saba turned, he began walking up and down the room, a sense of lightness and hope in his heart. If he had little chance with Alessandra, life still smiled on him. He felt healthy, strong, happy to be in the world, and ready to play his part, whether as protagonist, second lead, or extra, in whatever story life would decide to assign to him.

15

❧❦❧

AUGUST QUICKLY ENDED, and along with it, the vacation and Amos's hopes concerning Alessandra. The feverish desire to embrace her, to kiss her lips, to establish an intimacy with her would forever remain an unrealized dream. He tried to distract himself by thinking of the new things that awaited him at home. He knew that with the family away, the masons had worked almost without interruption. A splendid rectangular room had been finished—thirty feet by thirty-nine, with a fireplace open on all sides in the center of the room. The fireplace was made of brick and sat on a square base about eighteen inches high. Wrought-iron utensils were placed on an old millstone nearby. This design made starting a fire or cooking food easy.

Amos's father had also promised him a billiard table for this room. It would be placed under the big window that faced the rear. The last section of the old shed that had at one time been used to hold the harvest had been sacrificed to build this new room. Thus the entire house had been reconfigured to accommodate the family's needs. Amos's father liked to transform the house gradually and to see it become more and more elegant and functional. He had studied math and was happy to apply what he had learned to the house in which he was born, where his sons were born, and to which he felt deeply attached. When Amos entered the new room for the first time, he was excited. He opened the door cautiously, with the slowness of a poker player who draws the last card. Walking softly, he crossed the room and knelt down to touch the perfectly formed tiled floor, then approached the fireplace, enchanted by the originality of its construction.

Suddenly he thought of Alessandra. Amos felt a pain in his stomach, after which he imagined a great party held right here in this room. Alessandra would be by his side, along with his other friends. It really was the ideal place for such a party. His father, he was sure, would be happy for him to use the room that way, Amos thought. With this in mind, he turned and left by the door that opened out into the garden. The masons were still working on a small arcade, held up by squared columns of reinforced concrete; along the columns, the irregular lines left by the wood forms in which the cement was cast were visible. Amos leaned against a column, reflecting. For the first time the big country house seemed like a villa, a real villa. Along with the affection he had always had for the house, he now felt a new respect for it. He was truly fortunate to live in that house. His pleasure drove away any sense of uneasiness or malaise. Wheelbarrows full of fresh mortar and reddish-brown tiles arrived. The speed with which the masons worked made him feel healthy, energetic, anxious to be useful and to participate in this project, which he could see brought satisfaction to everyone: workers and family members alike.

"How's the voice? Let's hear you sing something!" said one of the workers. He dropped the handles of the wheelbarrow and turned toward Amos, his arms at his side. Amos smiled, walked across the garden to the palm that shaded the center of that small green space. Turning toward the arcade and in full voice, the veins standing out on his neck, he began to sing "La Mattinata," the celebrated aria by Leoncavallo: *"L'aurora di bianca vestita, / già l'uscio dischiude al gran sole."* The workmen stopped to listen to him, happy for this little diversion and the short rest it afforded them. Even the foreman, who usually never stopped working, put down his hammer and trowel to listen. After the final high note, there was a murmur of praise; then, returning to work, the men began talking about music. All of them agreed on the fact that one no longer heard songs as beautiful as those they remembered from their youth. "Even at the San Remo Festival," one of them was saying with a strong Tuscan accent, "one doesn't hear a good song!" Then, turning to Amos, he asked, "Why don't you go and make these clowns without a voice hear how to really sing?"

Amos had often heard this type of discussion, and it always made him happy to be the center of attention, the recipient of such praise. He reentered the house from the back of the kitchen and was about to open the glass doors that led to the first hallway when he heard strange voices coming from the breakfast room to his right. He stopped, curious to hear what was being said. Just at that moment the door to the room opened and Amos's grandmother, a bit surprised at seeing him there, invited him to enter. He was introduced to two young people, a man and a woman. "In fifteen days, they will be married," explained his grandmother, "and they would like you to sing for them at their wedding."

Amos didn't know what to say, so he smiled and remained silent. The groom-to-be intervened, addressing him and then his fiancée, from whom he seemed to ask silent confirmation of what he was saying. "We admire your voice; we even have a tape of you singing. Someone from our town gave it to us; he made it the night you sang at the theater in town, and we've always hoped that you would sing at our wedding."

Amos was silent. He certainly was not very enthusiastic about the invitation, but didn't want to decline, either. His grandmother spoke up then, begging him to consent. He smiled again and shyly said, "Okay."

That Sunday, dressed in his finest clothes, Amos made his way to the church half an hour before the Mass was due to begin. Passing the altar, he reached the choir, where the organist was waiting to rehearse. Then the invited guests began arriving a few at a time; the bride and the groom, however, were late. Amos sang at Communion, performing a piece that he had also sung at his brother's First Communion. Then, when the wedding vows had been exchanged and the newlyweds and the witnesses prepared to sign their names in the record book, he sang Schubert's "Ave Maria."

At the end of the ceremony, Amos shook many hands, kissed numerous elderly women who had been moved by the singing, bid farewell to the newlyweds, and received a gift from them. Finally, he returned home with his parents and grandmother, who was never absent from church on Sunday, even if she didn't feel well.

In the late afternoon, his friend Francesco Andreoli arrived from Bologna with his wife. He had met Francesco, who had a diploma in classical literature and taught at a school in Bologna, at the Cavazza Institute, and who had become fond of Amos. So he had accepted an invitation from Amos's father to spend a few days in the country and teach Amos the rudiments of Greek, a language he would soon be studying for the first time at his new school in Pontedera.

While in certain vineyards the harvest had already begun and the good smell of newly pressed grapes drifted in through the open windows of the house, Amos prepared for Greek. Study was a burden: it was one of those warm and luminous September days that make all outdoor activities and walks in the countryside so beautiful, and he would have preferred to be outside. The air wafting through the small study was rich with sounds and smells, but he tried to keep control of himself and show some interest in this ancient language that his parents and relatives had praised in an effort to persuade him to study the classics. Amos had a gift for languages, and was grateful that Francesco was willing to teach him, so he persevered. But it wasn't easy.

At the beginning of October, full of hopes and good intentions, Amos entered the classical school, together with two of his friends from the previous school. He was happy with the choice of a school and ready to begin his studies there. Unfortunately, as a famous Italian director used to say, "We often have many plans for the future, but they rarely coincide with the plans the future has for us." Things didn't go as Amos's friends and he had hoped. The fault lay with a young professor who taught Italian, Latin, Greek, history, and geography, for a total of almost twenty hours a week. She did not welcome someone like Amos, who needed special attention and teaching methods. She was irritated by his inability to read explanations written on the blackboard or to consult the dictionary by himself. She did not refrain from pointing out to the others that he was different, and he felt humiliated and discriminated against.

Sometimes she called on Amos in the middle of a lesson and, without mincing her words, would say, "Now, I would like you, or your mother, to explain to me how I can possibly send you to the blackboard to write and translate that sentence like all the other students."

Amos would remain silent, feeling embarrassed and full of shame. There was nothing, absolutely nothing, that he could do to combat the behavior of this presumptuous woman, for whom teaching was the only reason for living and who judged people solely on the basis of their apparent intelligence. She measured everything in terms of her own ego, which seemed so large it was almost pathological.

This woman sowed terror among her students. From the moment she entered the classroom until she left it, complete silence reigned; no one dared to whisper to a neighbor or pass a note; the atmosphere was such that some students even felt sick in class. Amos arrived at school every morning feeling increasingly sad, resigned, and alone, as well as certain that he could not succeed. During classwork, the teacher would call him to her desk so that no friend could help him use the dictionary. She demanded that he ask precise questions, indicating the exact nominative form of any given word. She pretended to ignore the fact that in looking in the dictionary one is searching for the *roots* of words.

After two months, Amos's psychological state had deteriorated badly, so much so that, to avoid the risk of failing, he gave in to the idea of quitting school altogether and transferring elsewhere, even though the year was already well under way. He was profoundly mortified by this decision and felt he was letting his family down, but he didn't see any alternative. Leaving school right away would mean he would not lose a year.

It was a defeat, but an honorable one. Amos's friends and family exerted themselves on his behalf, arranging a quick transfer to a teachers' institute. It was difficult to obtain a transfer at the start of the school year, and there had to be a valid reason for requesting such a transfer, but Amos swallowed his pride and accepted whatever had to be done to gain admission to a different school. His spirits were low and his enthusiasm completely gone. In this state of mind, Amos entered his new school, putting aside the most painful experience he had ever endured. He had learned a lesson from it, however: he now understood how a person's ignorance could harm a fellow human being.

Amos was fortunate to have an understanding family and the sympathy of his classmates, who, silently or openly, expressed support and kindness of a kind that until that moment he had not noticed. But his feeling of defeat remained; no one could get rid of that. It seemed as if his dreams would be thwarted by continuing limitations, humiliations, and bitterness, and the future looked bleak.

Entering an open gate in the small courtyard of the old building of this new school, Amos heard singing coming from a room on the second floor and was reminded that this school offered music lessons. His mother rang the bell, and a middle-aged woman appeared. She was short and fat and seemed out of breath, but she smiled cheerfully and let them in. Then, having called for the principal, she ran her hand through Amos's hair, wished them well, and returned to her work as custodian. Not far away, a young girl stood on the stairs, and Amos sensed that she was watching him. Although she had never seen him before, she had probably heard about him. As soon as she saw the principal, she turned and, with the lightness of a gazelle, Amos heard her take off.

Amos was escorted to his classroom and introduced to the other students, who seemed happy both with his arrival and the brief interruption in their morning's routine that it had caused. Then everything returned to normal and the literature professor resumed the lesson. As the bell for the last period rang, Amos panicked. He had to move to another room for French class and he didn't know whom to ask for help, or even which room to go to. Several of his classmates had already left the room, and others were gathering their things from their desks.

He was trying to decide what to do when a strong and decisive hand touched him on the shoulder. A calm, masculine voice—which seemed beautiful to him—full of warmth and goodwill, said, "My name is Adriano. Would you like to come with me to French class? I'd like to talk with you." Adriano took Amos's arm, guided him to the next class, and showed him where to sit. In those few minutes, a friendship was born.

Meeting Adriano changed Amos's life. First of all, the boy restored Amos's sense of humor, his faith in himself, and his trust in others; he even changed Amos's physical appearance. He encouraged him to abandon his elegant clothes—Prince of Wales trousers, camel-hair coats, white shirts with starched collars. He went shopping with Amos and they bought a pair of jeans. And Adriano showed him how to eliminate certain gestures that were typical of the blind. With his help, Amos soon felt like a different person.

Adriano was a lively boy, good at inventing jokes and thinking up fun ways to pass the time; he was cheerful, frank, and candid with everyone. In his circle, no one would dare undertake anything before hearing his opinion; his quips were often repeated and became very popular.

One day, Adriano and Amos went to a bar to have coffee; a friend joined them and began to tell Amos things about Adriano's childhood—escapades well known in Pontedera and still remembered.

"One morning," recalled the friend, "Adriano saw a horse tied to a cart full of stuff ready to be unloaded at a warehouse near his house. He was struck by the horse's enormous penis. He ran home, grabbed a small pistol that he had hidden in his room, lay in ambush, took aim, and shot the horse right in the penis. You can imagine what happened. The horse was enraged and turned over the cart. You should have heard the cursing of those men! They didn't know what had caused the animal to go crazy. Adriano ran home and told his mother not to open the door to anyone asking for a boy with a striped shirt. Then he hid under the bed." Adriano's silence confirmed the truth of the story, and they all burst into laughter. In the meantime, other children came over to listen.

Amos was doubled over, tears in his eyes from laughing so hard. After they left the bar, they agreed to go to Adriano's house to study. Amos was convinced that they would not accomplish much—lively as he was, Adriano certainly could not call himself a model student. He had already lost a year at the school and was again in danger of failing. But scholastic success is not always the best measure by which to gauge a person's worth. Adriano cared little for what Quintilian thought about the education of children; he was more concerned with understanding his fellow human beings and cultivating good friends. Teachers were the only people who did not like Adriano. They did not appreciate that he laughed at everything and everyone, even himself, and never took things very seriously. His teachers thought he acted superficial and nonchalant. They did not realize that sometimes the most serious things can be said only in jest, or else they seem boring, pretentious, and pedantic.

Adriano's life really deserves its own book, rich as it is in episodes that show his contradictory spirit, his sense of the absurd, his irony—qualities that many possess, but rarely in such a concentrated and striking way. Even back then, it was apparent that whatever road he chose to travel, no environment, no uniform, no professional injustice, no temptation to yield to corruption would compromise his integrity and frankness.

Amos knew then that he would never forget that big hand—dry and sure—that had rested on his shoulder, and the kindness Adriano showed him. Whenever he met him, it was always a pleasure to shake hands energetically.

Adriano was also well liked by the girls. Blessed with an athletic physique, pleasant features, and a friendly smile, he inspired feelings that ranged from physical attraction to an almost maternal tenderness. But deep down, Adriano was shy; he overcame his insecurity by being exuberant. Yet he also sought refuge in platonic relationships, full of poetry and ideals but lacking a feeling of true romance.

During the first days of school, Adriano fell in love with a girl called Barbara, who sat in the first row of one of his classes. She, however, never paid him much attention, perhaps because he never really declared himself and because she was attracted to older boys. Adriano suffered a lot because of these unrequited longings, and confiding in Amos, he spoke of her in the most flattering terms—so much so that Amos ended up falling in love with her, too. He immediately confessed his feelings to Adriano and they both began, in an atmosphere of complete loyalty, an assiduous practice of courting her, although very properly.

Barbara felt flattered by all this attention, but she had a twenty-two-year-old boyfriend, who often came to get her at school and took her home in his car. So, hopes of the boys' winning her were reduced to almost nothing; even so, they liked to nurture those hopes and spent time building castles in the air.

Barbara was short, dark, and had long hair; she was pretty and shapely, but it was her luminous and expressive face that was most beguiling. She was always smiling. She had large eyes, an intense gaze, an elegant nose, and dimples, which made her smile that much more radiant. Amos could visualize just what she looked like because Adriano had described her to him. Both boys loved her with a chaste and pure love, which excluded vulgar thoughts and words.

One afternoon, at the end of a conversation about Barbara, Adriano rose, quickly left the room, and returned with a guitar that he barely knew how to strum. He sat down and told Amos to pay attention; although skeptical, Amos prepared to listen. Adriano pulled a small plectrum from the pocket of his shirt and plucked the strings, producing a chord in A minor (one of the few that he knew), after which he began to sing a song that Amos had never heard but that seemed sweet and full of feeling.

When it was finished, Adriano explained with some emotion that he had written it himself, for Barbara. Incredulous but sincerely touched, Amos asked to hear it again. Before he left, he wanted to write down the words so that he could take them home and ruminate over them as if they were his own.

> *Mi ricordo quella notte sulla spiaggia,*
> *illuminata dal tuo sguardo verso l'infinito.*

> *I remember that night at the beach,*
> *illuminated by your glance toward infinity . . .*

Was it a dream, or had Adriano really spent a night with her at the beach? Amos wondered. To him, those words seemed full of poetry. And it was so true: Barbara's look *could* illuminate any darkness! He was moved by another passage, as well:

> *Come un gabbiano sperduto*
> *cerca l'azzuro del mare,*
> *io nei tuoi occhi l'amore.*

As a lost seagull
seeks the blue of the sea,
I seek love in your blue eyes.

Those simple words surged from an enamored and wounded heart, just like Amos's own; repeating them, he felt a shiver throughout his body.

Bravo, Adriano, Amos thought, unable to understand how such a delicate artistic sensibility could exist in a person so completely devoid of musical talent. He felt admiration for Adriano, but no jealousy, as envy was a quality completely lacking in their friendship. Amos soon began to idealize Adriano, and defended him with the almost fanatical zeal that teenagers often feel.

16

DESPITE AMOS'S FREE and easy manner of dressing and behavior, his relationship with the opposite sex remained an unresolved problem. Amos had grown to be a tall boy with very black hair, a not uncommon look with strong features, large shoulders, and long, muscular legs: in short, he could not be said to be displeasing to the eye; and yet he could not manage to attract the attention of his female classmates, especially those he was interested in. Forcing himself to analyze the situation, he became aware that his sometimes exasperated attempts to please made him a bit clumsy and awkward; then there was his disability, which did the rest. It was necessary therefore to resign himself to the facts; perhaps the best thing to do would be to concentrate on something else, something that, with the passage of time, would make him more interesting, more sure of himself, more of a man. What Amos could neither explain nor accept was the seeming success with girls of some of his classmates, who appeared empty, disagreeable, lacking any humanity, and totally incapable of pursuing an ideal. He would meet them on the streets of Pontedera or somewhere else, arm in arm with beautiful girls. How could they have won the hearts of young girls who seemed so kind?

What a strange comedy life is, he thought as he struggled to grasp the rules, and understand the way the world works; but the more he tried the less he succeeded, and he lost himself in the labyrinth of his thoughts, intentions, and hopes. Although Amos suffered, he did not despair: a strange indefinable presentiment prompted him to remain strong, to wait with faith, to be optimistic. After all, nothing prevented him from enjoying what he had: the affection of friends and family, physical well-being, the progress he was making . . . All in all, he thought, I have nothing to complain about: there are so many people worse off than me. He forced himself not to think about what was missing, to minimize every problem, every difficulty, every obstacle.

True, the idea that Barbara turned her attentions to others made him feel ill. Every morning Amos woke up with the idea of soon seeing her and speaking to her; a kind gesture, a word from her, was sufficient to plant a dream in his heart, a hope that he would dwell on for days and days, usually listening to music; music that he loved also because it helped him withdraw into himself, to remain alone with his own thoughts.

One afternoon, while listening to a tape of *Cavalleria Rusticana* and reading a poem by Gozzano at the same time, Amos felt an undeniable need to compose a poem for Barbara, just as had happened when he was pining over Alessandra. This time, though, he didn't think about reciting the lines to her; he would keep the poem to himself, for his own pleasure. He closed the book, switched off his tape, took his typewriter, and in no time typed:

To leave everything and run far away, far from the gaze of people,
from this life of mine made of nothing, to escape, holding you by the hand.

Then finally alone in a street, conquered by the same desires,
Defeated by the most sincere feelings, lost in a tender folly:

To love each other there! Crazy for you and covering you first with kisses
*   chaste then prohibited,*
Seeking your skin beneath the clothes and enfolding you in sensual caresses.

But the dream lasts a moment and vanishes and I remain the foolish dreamer,
*   who believes in the fable of love;*
That which enchants, deludes, then ends . . .

Who knows from where the sound of a sad bell reaches me to announce the
*   evening;*
I am alone and you are farther away than the bell, and the soul despairs.

Is it cowardice? Hypochondria? What is it that grasps my heart like pincers?
What is this anxiety of mine, this battle, that unchains in me so much fury
when I think of you, and quickly my senses inflame, so that suddenly I miss
*   your kisses, your smile,*
And my desires intensify?

Dismayed, I ask myself if you think of me, my love, who you carry in your
*   heart;*
And as one day dies and another arrives, I still love you.

After writing the last verse, he realized that he had not thought of a title. That detail did not seem especially important to him; still, he rolled the bar of the typewriter to the top of the page and wrote the first thing that came to mind. The title was "Sogno" (Dream). He recited those verses out loud to see if they sounded good; they weren't much compared with the lyrics of Gozzano, yet he liked them, and felt he should be indulgent with himself. He folded the paper, hid it between the pages of his encyclopedia, and went out for a breath of air.

It was sunset, a spring sunset. The air was mild and the light breeze that wafted from the west—from the sea—carried the delicate scent of nature, awakening from the sleep of winter and dressing in delicate blooms. Amos breathed deeply: together with the air, a new energy, penetrating his nostrils, entered him and spread throughout his body; a longing for movement, and to think and transmit his thoughts to others. He felt the need of a friend to help, an enemy to fight, an idea in which to believe, others to reject; in short, he felt a need to *do* something, to *complete* something that he would later be able to contemplate, with the satisfaction of one who can say: "This is my work."

He began to run until he reached a nearby house. Sergio, a cousin whom he had known all his life, was fooling around with a motorbike. The two boys talked briefly; then Sergio washed his hands and the two of them set off toward town, on a bike licensed to carry only one person, without any precise plan.

Reaching the piazza, they parked and walked toward the small youth club. It was a small two-room apartment with a bathroom. In the first room there was a big secondhand bench, some small tables with chairs, a pinball machine, a television, and a freezer for ice cream: in short, only the things absolutely necessary for a bar; in the second there were a few couches and armchairs, and a stereo system. The two rooms were connected: the only barrier was a curtain that had been hung haphazardly, almost to the ceiling. Anyone who wished to enter pulled the curtain aside and passed through; entering the other room, one often became the indiscreet witness to one or more couples, whose privacy was defended only by the semidarkness of that room and the volume, usually high, of the stereo system.

Amos climbed the small steps outside the club, which he knew from memory as though they were the steps of his own house. He entered and soon realized that something was going on. A boy approached him, greeted him, and told him that it still was possible to sign up for the chess tournament. There were a good number of people in the place and an air of great excitement.

Sergio, who wasn't interested in chess, left Amos and went to the sports club. He said he would pass by later and accompany Amos home, in time for supper. Amos signed up for the tournament, then went to sit at a table with some other kids who were already playing. He wanted to check out their skills.

A girl approached him, placed her hand on his, and greeted

him cordially. Amos would have liked to have her sit down next to him, but the chairs were all occupied and so the girl remained standing. So Amos got up and gestured that she take his seat, but she turned him around and sat on his knee. Helped by the relaxed atmosphere of the tournament and the conversations about chess, Amos acted with a naturalness that for him was a novelty. He spoke to the girl about opening gambits, game plans, final moves, strategy, the philosophy of play; she pretended to be interested, but Amos felt strange about the way she was seated on his knees. A sensation he had never felt before deeply disturbed him; so much so that he lost the thread of the conversation.

The girl got up from his lap and went to the adjoining room, turning on the record player and arranging a stack of records to fall automatically onto the turntable, allowing for continuous music. She sat on a couch and got ready to listen.

Antonella, which was the girl's name, was happy and intelligent, and although she studied at the *liceo,* she did not try to hide her country-girl origins; her behavior and language had remained those of the world in which she had grown up. She could not be described as a beauty: she was very short, with a few extra pounds and large breasts, but Amos could tell that her face was animated, and she displayed an irresistible kindness. She was dedicated to her studies, and her academic achievements were considerable, but she also found time to enjoy herself. She was frank, direct, and without prejudices. She liked boys and they flocked to her, attracted by her femininity and sensuality. Many in town had courted her with success; even so, she was not the butt of jokes or gossip. She was respected, as people who know their business are respected.

After five or ten minutes, Antonella returned to Amos's table. She stopped in front of him and asked him to follow her to listen to some music. Amos had a moment's hesitation, but she grabbed him by the hand and pulled him up. The curtain fell on their shoulders as they passed into the other room. They sat down on the couch. Amos, embarrassed, began talking of the first subject that crossed his mind. For a while she listened to him patiently, then she moved her face closer to him, almost touching his, and said: "I like to listen to you, but I'd prefer to look at you, if you'll only keep quiet for a minute."

Then she kissed him. It was a long and deep kiss. Amos found himself wishing it would never end.

❧❧

Time passed and the kids left the club for supper. By eight o'clock there was no one left. When Amos awoke from his dream he asked Antonella what time it was. She glanced at her watch and answered, "It's nine o'clock; why, are you hungry?" Amos wasn't hungry but was worried about his parents, who were probably looking for him. Yet he felt strong, courageous, ready to confront any problem. He tried to take stock of the situation: although everything had not happened, *enough* had happened. After that experience he felt different. He felt like a man. He felt capable of confronting any problem. He brushed aside the curtain, took a bottle and two glasses from the table outside, opened the cash register, paid, and sat at a table with his new friend.

What feeling is this? he thought to himself. Certainly it was a different type of love than what he felt for Barbara: less ideal but much more concrete. He also thought, Why hasn't Sergio come by for me? What could have happened? Sergio *had* passed by, but seeing how things were going, he didn't want to disturb Amos; wisely he had telephoned Amos's parents to inform them that their son was staying in town for the chess tournament and would eat at a friend's house. But that night Amos ate absolutely nothing: he wasn't hungry and there wasn't even time to eat. The kids were slowly returning to the club and soon the tournament would begin.

His first adversary was not a problem for Amos. He barely knew the moves and within half an hour he had surrendered. But the second adversary was one of the best. A medical student who had almost completed his degree, this guy had dedicated himself ruthlessly to chess. Amos had already played him several times and the results were not in his favor. In addition, Amos was distracted and poorly motivated: his mind went back to the extraordinary events of earlier that day.

The chessboard he had before him seemed strange and far away. He played the opening he knew best—the King's—but after about twenty moves committed a silly error and lost a piece. When he realized there wasn't much of a match anymore, he rose, sportingly offered his hand to his opponent, said good-bye, and left with Sergio, who had come back with the other kids, to return home. In other circumstances he would have felt dejected and demoralized; but not that night. He couldn't wait to see Adriano and to recount his day, to discuss with him the experience he had had. He was proud of what had happened; it seemed to him an important step toward what he called "normality," notwithstanding the doubts that some—not he!—had held.

Amos reached home excited but exhausted. His parents were already in bed. He raced up the stairs, and before reaching his room heard his father's voice, which said in a reproving tone: "Is this any hour to come home? How will you get up tomorrow morning?" Amos didn't answer. He quickly undressed, got into bed, and pulled the sheets up to his chin, and soon after fell into such a deep sleep that not even dreams found a way to disturb him.

17

※❦※

THE YEARS AMOS spent at the school of Pontedera were a period of true daydreaming. He had thought that his encounter with Antonella would signal a turning point, but it wasn't like that at all: Amos continued to oscillate between two poles, Barbara and Adriano, the cross and the delight of his life. Perhaps Barbara appreciated him, perhaps she recognized in him some good qualities; she demonstrated her esteem when she voted for him as class representative. But she did not love him and Amos would have preferred her love to her esteem. Adriano, though, was a friend in a way that Amos liked best. His presence inspired Amos and allowed him to formulate his opinions, some of which would otherwise have remained vague and incomplete. He was the only one to whom Amos dared confess everything, certain of being understood, if not always approved of.

It was during those years that a conviction, which turned into a whole philosophy of life, slowly developed in Amos. The conviction was this: every man distinguishes himself by his unique qualities, but all men resemble each other in their defects, which are universal. Slowly, this thought directed Amos toward tolerance and understanding: it was a long, difficult, and tortuous process, because it forced him to restrain his impulsive and passionate character.

Having earned her degree, the young woman who tutored Amos every day in his homework and reading had decided to marry a young man from the town. Replacing her was a problem, but it was rather urgent to do so because that year Amos was to take the final exams leading to his degree. It wasn't easy to find an alert and capable young woman who could quickly get to know Amos, his difficulties and needs, and who could master his way of learning. Everyone in the family was concerned and tried to seek out information and find a solution.

During a sleepless night, the answer came to Mrs. Bardi in the name of Ettore. Ettore was neither a college graduate nor a teacher, and he was fifty-five years old; and yet Amos's mother thought that he might be the best solution. But to convince him would be difficult.

Recently, Ettore had retired as director of the Banca Popolare e Agricola of Lajatico: everyone thought it was too early a retirement for a man of his age and energy. Ettore was a singular person, with extraordinary intellectual gifts and human qualities, still healthy and strong. He seemed to be ten years younger than his years. How could such a lively and energetic man, so full of life, interests, and goodwill remain inactive?

One might expect anything from him, thought Mrs. Bardi. With a book in hand he was always happy. He liked to walk in the countryside and forests, looking for mushrooms or snails, or simply contemplating nature. And he liked to travel; he and his wife had traveled all over the world. Perhaps now that he was free, he would take the opportunity to go on other trips, moved by his unquenchable thirst to learn, to experience everything himself.

He was a strange man. When the management of the bank had informed him of its intention to promote him to director, he calmly accepted the offer but neglected to request a raise in salary; instead he had asked, with a few simple words that were not without irony, if he could keep his rank as employee. The president of the bank, a bit stupefied by the extravagant request, did not let the opportunity pass by. Ettore was a man outside the norm, but every-one respected him for his capabilities and for his generosity in advising and helping those in need.

Mrs. Bardi asked herself if he would consider the idea of lend-ing a hand with her son's studies. The idea was bizarre, but so was Ettore, and perhaps it was the very strangeness of the request that would induce him to accept. But Mrs. Bardi didn't know how to formulate the question. A too direct approach might ruin every-thing. Better a more gentle inquiry.

Mrs. Bardi said a brief prayer to God, switched on the light, and looked at her bedside clock. It was 6 A.M. She got up, got dressed, and went down to the kitchen. She remembered that that day she had an appointment with a client at Poggioncino who wanted to discuss the eventual purchase of a tractor. She made breakfast, climbed into the car, and made her way toward Lajatico. In the piazza she glanced at her watch: it was already almost 7:30. She turned right onto the Via Garibaldi. The bar was already open and she saw several pupils enter, and others leaving with small snacks for school. She looked ahead, and a few dozen yards away saw Ettore, who was walking quickly in her direction, with a pencil in one hand and a crumpled piece of paper in the other. She watched him, wondered whether to stop him, passed him, but farther on she slowed down, reversed, and returned to the piazza. Ettore was lin-gering in front of a newspaper kiosk. Mrs. Bardi parked the car, climbed out, and caught up with him just as he was leaving with a pair of daily newspapers under his arm and a third that he was leaf-ing through. She greeted him, and he distractedly returned the greeting, but when he realized that Mrs. Bardi had something to say to him, he closed the newspaper and was ready to listen to her. "I need your help," Mrs. Bardi began. Ettore smiled, and she contin-ued: "My son is to take the graduation exams this year, and the young woman who was helping him is leaving to get married . . ."

Ettore blushed and appeared embarrassed. "So now you would like—" he murmured.

Mrs. Bardi interrupted him resolutely: "Yes, I am sure that you are the only person capable of helping him." Then, "Of course," she added, "you must give us an idea of your fee."

This last sentence, of course, sounded a bit awkward and inelegant, but it had one good effect: that of shaking Ettore out of his shyness. He answered in an angry voice, "If you so much as speak to me again of such a thing, signora, you will force me to abandon the project." Did that mean, perhaps, that he had accepted?

There was a moment of silence, then Ettore said with a smile, "Okay, but do not expect too much just yet; I don't know if I will be capable."

He glanced again at the first pages of the newspaper and concluded, "Today at five I will be at your house." He said good-bye, turned, and slowly walked toward the church, immersed in his reading.

Perhaps for the first time in her life Mrs. Bardi forgot about business and returned home straightaway to tell her husband about what seemed to her a great victory. Her maternal instinct told her that what had just happened was a real piece of good luck for Amos. She found her husband at the front door of the house, ready to leave. She made him go back inside, sat down, and with the enthusiasm of a schoolgirl spoke to him of her sleepless nights, the bizarre project that had all of a sudden burst into her head, and her encounter with Ettore.

Mr. Bardi listened and at the end declared himself truly surprised. He knew Ettore well, and during the last few years had had reason to visit him often, having been elected trustee to the board of the bank, and then vice-president. He admitted that he would have laughed at the idea if his wife had consulted him. "But are you sure you understood him right? It seems very strange to me that he accepted. He's so introverted . . . some even say odd . . ."

"You never change!" answered Mrs. Bardi, a bit annoyed by her husband's skepticism. "You doubt everything. Just you wait and see!"

"I can't imagine that he'll stay for long. What with your son's character, he'll be leaving after half an hour!"

That's what Amos's father said, but one could see the joy and satisfaction on his face. Finally, he and his wife decided to go out, but for the entire morning they continued discussing Ettore and whether he would get along with Amos when the boy returned from school. Ettore and Amos had always known of each other, but their contact had been minimal, even insignificant. It was difficult to guess how things might turn out between the two of them.

"Whatever happens, happens," Mr. Bardi would say, laughing, every time he caught a glance from Mrs. Bardi.

"It's going to be great!" she answered, displaying her characteristic optimism.

❦

That day at lunch every member of the Bardi family was present. They waited for the return of the boys from school, and when everyone was seated, Mrs. Bardi announced to Amos that Mr. Ettore, ex-director of the bank, had agreed to help him in his studies, at least until the exams. Amos heard the news calmly, almost indifferently. At the end of the meal, Mr. Bardi rose from the table and invited his son to follow him into the breakfast room. "Are you happy about this?" he asked, and then, without waiting for an answer began to praise Ettore.

"You don't really know him. He's a strange man, but really exceptional. Just think, he directed our town bank with only a little education. When he attended meetings with the directors of larger banks, he was almost always silent, but if he spoke everyone listened to him with respect and no one dared to contradict him, because they knew that he never said anything that he was not sure of. Apparently, he's capable of reading and writing at least six languages. He knows French, English, and Russian well—just think, Russian!—and he gets by in Spanish and German, too. He reads continuously and no one has ever found him to be lacking in knowledge on any subject. It seems impossible, but it's true. In elementary school he was a pupil of Aunt Leda's, and she has always spoken of him as an extraordinarily gifted child: something that's even more surprising if one thinks that he comes from a very poor family. His father was a mason and his mother a maid. They lived in direst poverty, yet Ettore became the director of a bank and he could have gone even further, with his intelligence and capabilities. But he's not very sociable; he loves to be on his own, and always goes his own way. So try to behave yourself with him. Every once in a while your mother has a good idea!"

He laughed, and then added, "Pay very close attention to how you speak, because if your grammar is poor or you use slang, you will make a bad impression. Nothing escapes him."

Amos listened to his father in silence. The description of Ettore reassured him, and made him curious.

"Okay," he said. He got up and together with his father left the room. He called a friend on the phone and talked about nonsense, forgetting about Ettore, exams, and homework. It was so like Amos to bury away thoughts and worries until the moment arrived when it was necessary to dig them up again.

18

✤✤✤

ETTORE ARRIVED TEN MINUTES EARLY, parked his
car under the two tall pines trees close to the house, and rang the
bell. Amos, who had been waiting for him, went to open the door.
Their introduction was brief: a handshake, then Ettore greeted the
rest of the family and asked to be shown to Amos's study. He was
curious to understand—as he said—what help he could give. Amos
showed him his books and the tape recorder on which Ettore was
to record his voice so that Amos could study even when he was
alone. Ettore smiled, partly from embarrassment, partly from
enjoyment: "I have never read out loud in my life, but I'll do my
best," he said.

Then they were left alone. The door of the study closed behind
Grandmother Leda, who was the last to exit the room, after leaving
a tray with a coffeepot, sugar bowl, cups, and espresso spoons.

After exchanging pleasantries, Ettore opened a history book
while Amos put a reel on the tape recorder, which, thanks to its
four tracks and double speed, could tape for sixteen hours. "So, let's
begin to fill up that tape, eh?" said Ettore, and he quickly began to
read the first chapter, all about the Congress of Vienna. He read
and read, not without hesitation but without stopping, and then
he closed the book and invited Amos to stop the tape.

"It would be a good idea at this point," he said, "to discuss what we have read, to see if everything is clear, or if I can help you understand something that has escaped you."

Amos had not been paying close attention, and Ettore realized that he'd have to explain everything all over from the beginning. He did this with patience. At the end of the scheduled two hours, he rose and promised to return the next afternoon at the same time. Crossing the breakfast room to leave, he saw a chessboard on the table.

"Do you like to play?"

"Yes, I am a *passionist,*" Amos answered him, proud to be able to show off his ability, and to use a word that seemed appropriate and rare. Ettore smiled, good-naturedly. He looked at Amos and said:

"You may be an *appassionato,* but I don't believe you belong to an order of passionist friars!"

He started to speak of that order, of its founder, its develop-ment, of the passionists who had distinguished themselves for one reason or another. He gave the impression of there being a great congestion of ideas that crowded in his head and furiously fought with each other to escape. Amos was amazed by all that erudition and let Ettore exhaust the subject without saying a word himself. Then he laughed, though his feelings were slightly hurt. He was reminded of what his father had told him only a few hours earlier. And to think that he had spoken so little and listened so carefully to avoid uttering something stupid!

From that moment Amos felt an immature desire to catch Ettore in some error, to even the score, but he soon realized it was impossible. In their arguments, he was always wrong. When Ettore wasn't able to persuade his young pupil about some point or other and Amos would dig in his heels and refuse to concede, Ettore would get up from the chair, go to the bookshelves, pull out an encyclopedia or sometimes a dictionary or a book of essays, open it, and smiling, he would show Amos his error; then he would replace the book and not speak of the subject again, putting aside the victory without even taking the satisfaction of mocking him.

Amos's admiration and gratitude grew day by day. Ettore made him question everything; he dismantled every certainty, every preconception, every form of youthful fanaticism, but at the same time he instilled the seeds of doubt, a procedure that at first provokes anguish and bewilderment, but later strengthens and gives joy. Doubting not only helps one to grow but frees one from the obligation of always being right at all costs—which is a form of slavery. Paradoxically, one is more often right when one doesn't *desire* too much to be right.

A sense of equanimity and peace grew little by little in Amos, something he had not felt before. From Ettore, Amos never received praise or signs of esteem, and yet he felt for him an affection that rapidly grew, fed by the strength and dedication of that strange instructor.

During a walk along the river one day, Ettore said: "One needs great power to produce both good and evil, but to do good one needs much more, because goodness is to evil like building is to destroying, and the first is much more demanding than the second; good and evil are in the hands of the powerful, but those who do good are greater, even if they don't often get noticed and work in the shadows. Remember that humanity advances on their shoulders."

Amos would never forget his words. He listened and knew that he shared these ideas. He made them his own, and was pleased with the response they elicited every time he repeated them to others. He seemed to be growing in people's estimation as he had never dared hope. More and more, people asked him his views and wanted to know his opinion on all kinds of things.

Meanwhile, another set of exams was approaching, and Amos was becoming more and more anxious. Ettore increased his visits, and lengthened them to four or five hours every afternoon, and then he even started to come on Sunday mornings. He tried to help Amos keep things in proportion: "These are things that one must take seriously, but one mustn't make them into matters of life and death. There are other, more important matters in this world. Therefore, study hard, but don't make a mountain out of a mole-hill."

Amos studied with all his strength, in spite of the springtime, the thousand distractions, his other interests—horses, music, and so on—and his love for Barbara, which remained unresolved.

At long last the first day of exams arrived. After attendance had been called, Amos was led into a separate room so that he could work without disturbing the other students; then an instructor came to give him the topics. Leaving, he wished Amos good luck and closed the door behind him. Amos chose the topic that concerned pedagogy. He had to comment on a passage by Quintilian about the importance of the "spirit of competition" among children in their first years of study. Amos thought that most of his classmates would argue for the spirit of the group rather than the individual, and would prefer a school that aimed more to *form* rather than *inform,* that educated more for cooperation than for competition, and that prepared its students to integrate well into society rather than one that focused solely on individual capabilities. Amos decided to take a risk and to say what he thought. He began by stressing the fundamental importance of the relationship between the student and the teacher; supporting his thesis with references to John Dewey, Maria Montessori, and others. He held that the relationship must single out the natural inclinations of every student and direct them in such a way as to create coherent personalities, capable of making themselves useful both to their families and to the world of work; in short, to be good citizens. In this light, competitiveness becomes fundamental: it fuels human will, ignites the imagination, develops the mind and its creative gifts. With competition there comes a desire for a just and morally unimpeachable victory, because he who struggles to win gives the best of himself and sets goals that translate into benefits for all . . . He who struggles to win understands that the objective is not to triumph over others, but rather for the triumph of his freedom to express itself and transform itself into an example worth imitating.

Amos believed in what he was writing; for this reason, the writing came easily to him and he didn't even need to recopy the essay in better handwriting. He finished early, rose, and left the room to ask if someone would come and get his paper. Then he went out into the *piazzale* where his mother was waiting for him, anxious to know how he thought he'd done.

When he had finished the written exams, Amos concentrated on the oral exams. He had chosen to be tested in philosophy first, in the hope that history would be chosen second. His hopes were not in vain. When he heard his name read out, he entered the exam hall. He felt a tension that he was not able to overcome. He sat down, clenched his fists, breathed deeply, and waited for the questions.

Amos was questioned first on Kantian ethics, then on Marx and Engels. He had written a small essay for his teacher on *Das Kapital*—the very work of the founder of communism—and so he felt touched by fortune and responded easily. Even the history exam was a success. It had been Ettore who had read to him and commented on the textbook, but Amos embellished his answers with accounts of fascism and the Second World War that he had heard from various people, and this had made him so passionate and interested in the subject that he loved history more than any other subject.

At the end of the orals, the head of the examining committee handed back his written work, congratulating him on an excellent exam, which the professor who had graded it had not even corrected. Amos triumphantly left the school, never to return, and waited confidently for the results.

He got the highest possible grade: sixty out of sixty. Exultant, he telephoned Ettore to share the triumph with him. Ettore let

him speak, then laughed and said that the committee had definitely gone easy on him: "Forty, yes, maybe you deserved a forty,
but not more!" But it was obvious that even he was satisfied.

❧

It was necessary then to look ahead and to think about the future.
The next morning, at precisely ten o'clock, Ettore was at Amos's
house with his motorbike and a nylon bag that contained a couple
of books and a newspaper.

"So, have you decided what to do?" he asked.

"What do you want me to do? I will enroll in the Anno Integrativo [a basic law course] and then in law school; this way I'll
have time to think about my future. There are many lawyers in my
family, and everyone has always expected me to follow in their
footsteps. I was still a child when they started telling me that I
would be a lawyer. So with the passage of time, I started to believe
it a bit myself. Then came the diploma. If the exams hadn't gone
so well, maybe I would have studied an instrument, for example, I
would have finished piano studies. But now . . ."

Ettore made no comment: after offering to accompany Amos
to Pisa to enroll in the Anno Integrativo, he proposed that they
leaf through the newspaper. This was a habit that Amos had never
acquired, until then.

In the following days, Ettore made another suggestion to
Amos: to read *The Leopard* by Tomasi di Lampedusa. Amos loved
that book, and in that sticky heat of summer he felt a renewed
interest in fiction being born in himself. An interest that brought
him back to those serene evenings in which Uncle Comparini had
read novels to him, distracting him from the television, which his
uncle called "that ungrateful and troublesome guest."

Ettore read out loud, with less embarrassment than a few
months before, and he never tired of adding comments and explanations. The time flew by each evening, and when Ettore left,

Amos felt a sense of solitude. He would ponder their readings and it seemed to him that he was growing in spirit. This growth manifested itself in new things to say and a greater facility of expression. Now there were many more things that interested him, and this made him less bored and lazy.

After *The Leopard* he learned to love the Russian classics. He began with Gogol and read *Dead Souls*. Then he fell in love with Dostoyevsky. Reading *The Brothers Karamazov* and above all *Crime and Punishment* made him feel like a different person. After these he threw himself into reading Tolstoy and finished *War and Peace* in a few nights. He spoke of it with real enthusiasm to his friends and was stunned when he realized that none of them had read it in its entirety, and many had not even read a single line.

In the meantime he attended the so-called Anno Integrativo, that would allow him to enroll in law school. The strange afternoon classes were not very demanding, and not very interesting. Speaking about the class with friends, Amos described it as a real waste of time, just like military service. The Anno Integrativo left him with a lot of free time, which Amos spent with friends, playing games, reading, and indulging in his usual pastimes.

It was around this time that Sergio took Amos by motorbike to Marica's house. She was a girl he had heard a lot about. Marica attended the professional institute, where Sergio had met her, and she hoped to find a position as a secretary at some firm. She was a tall, slim girl, with long chestnut hair that framed a sweet face with features that were nearly perfect; her legs were so long that they almost seemed out of proportion to the rest of her body. But what really got under Amos's skin was Marica's voice; smooth and subtle, calm and very feminine; the voice of a siren. Amos loitered for as long as possible, and when he said good-bye he invited her to his house, saying they could listen to some records. He questioned her and learned that she had little interest in music. Even so, Marica accepted the invitation, and Amos, returning home, tried to understand the reasons for her acquiescence and asked himself how he could entertain Marica and conquer the young beauty's heart.

Amos's emotional affairs were never simple things, and he was rather amazed that such a popular and, at least at first sight, slightly superficial girl (even though he was emotionally involved, Amos made some concession to objectivity) would be interested in him. He didn't know that Sergio, ever the altruist, had spoken to her of his family, his property, and his horses, to make Amos sound good: these things had probably sparked a curiosity in the girl to visit the villa and to see up close how the "other half" lived.

Amos had shaken her hand; she found him kind, polite, and mature. Observing him closely, she had even thought him handsome, and was not troubled by the fact that he couldn't see her. In her small room that night, cluttered with the usual female knickknacks, Marica tried to imagine Amos's room and the living room that Sergio had described, the comfortable sofas where perhaps Amos would sit her down and take her hand . . .

A few days went by and Marica kept her promise. When Amos went to open the door, he was truly surprised to find her standing before him, but she was not embarrassed at all, and Amos quickly felt at ease with her. He introduced her to Delfina, the woman who had taken the place of Oriana when she had married, and who now helped the Bardi family in cleaning the house. Then he invited Marica to follow him into the living room, and as she had imagined, he had her sit down. He began to play a recording of some Italian popular music; finally, he sat down next to her, and so they remained for nearly the entire afternoon. When she left, they already shared a sweet secret, the displeasure of having to leave each other and the desire to meet again as soon as possible.

Marica became Amos's girlfriend: his first. He introduced her to his friends, who welcomed her warmly: everyone was pleased to see him so happy. Eventually Amos would cease showing up alone at bars, meals, or nightclubs, as he had always done before.

At the beginning of the summer, Amos passed the exams set by the Anno Integrativo. It was a mere formality.

❧⁙❧

After six months Amos and Marica were still together. Their relationship began to be very important to both of them. Life grants sweet experiences and sometimes deceptive ones, and both Amos and Marica could point to such experiences in their love story. They passed the entire summer together. They saw each other every day and Amos threw himself into the relationship with all the ardor of his impetuous character. He was never tired of holding her in his arms, and she adored being the object of such great desire. They loved each other, or perhaps it is more exact to say that they desired each other. Neither of them placed a check on their own desire, or on that of the other.

November arrived and Amos, who had enrolled in law school, began to attend classes together with Eugenio, his old friend from school. Both of them decided to begin their university adventure quickly, by preparing for the most complicated of the six first-year exams: that of private law. Ettore had a hard time of it in describing to Amos the required essentials and the incidental elements of contracts, titles of credit, and succession. Amos had moments of great discouragement, but Ettore was always there, ready to encourage him and to try to convince him that, in certain cases, it is not so much simple memory that saves you but the ability to reason about things.

"What counts," he would say, "is to understand what has guided the *thinking* of the lawmaker; memory only lets you down if it is not sustained by reasoning. And remember," he would continue, "*nemo censetur ignorare legem;* and if no one is allowed to plead ignorance of the law, you who have enrolled in law school will have even less cause to plead ignorance. Your grades won't be as good as some students who memorize everything but who have understood nothing—but of what importance is that? What counts is to understand and to go forward."

It was around that time that Ettore introduced Amos to French literature of the nineteenth and twentieth centuries. After passing the first big exam without excelling but without embarrassing himself either, Amos began to read and love the French authors, Flaubert first and then Maupassant, Zola, Mauriac, Balzac, Sartre . . . he read and discussed with Ettore his impressions, he accepted suggestions on new things to read, and book by book, he became more and more passionate about literature and less so about his law studies, which he continued to do sluggishly and without enthusiasm. Through the novels he seemed to better understand the innate *sense* of life; with his law studies, he was interested only in the theoretical aspects; technical and practical aspects—so important for one who wishes to be a lawyer—awakened absolutely no interest in him.

Without any great effort he completed the exams in political economy, Roman law, public law, and civil law; more willingly and with the highest possible grade, he sailed through the exam in philosophy of law: a subject which, compared with the others, seemed to him to be really alive and intellectually stimulating; so much so that he decided he would approach the professor who taught the class when it came time to decide on a subject for his thesis.

He had completed the first-year exams with fair grades. In the meantime Marica had graduated and had found work as a secretary in a home-furnishings store. Amos felt a secret jealousy, which he dared not confess even to himself. He understood that he could not stop Marica from working, but even so he suffered, thinking of all the men who would approach her. And if she succumbed? To Amos this thought was unbearable. Correctly guessing his worries, Ettore laughed at him. "So then you're an old-fashioned man," he would say, and he tried to cheer him up. "You walk around with such a flashy girl at your side and pretend that others ignore her!

And how do *you* act when you meet a beautiful girl who is already committed to someone else?"

Amos didn't respond, but his entire being rebelled at the situation.

❧

One Saturday afternoon Marica seemed a bit different from usual; they had gone for a walk by the river and she was silent and serious, perhaps even sad. Amos asked why. After some resistance, the girl admitted that an episode that had occurred the previous day had greatly disturbed her.

"I was in my office," she began, "and just before I finished work, my boss came in. He sat down in front of me, chatted about work a little, and then asked me point-blank to go out to dinner with him. I said nothing—though he could tell from my expression what I was thinking—and he quickly added that he intended only to speak to me about work. I replied that I was not permitted to come home late; so then he offered to call my parents. I was very embarrassed, but after thinking about it for a bit, I said we could perhaps get something to eat at the bar nearby some evening. He glanced at his watch and said that he considered my work finished for the day. He said we could leave immediately. At the bar we sat at a small table, we ordered something to drink, and then, to cut a long story short, after complimenting me on my skills as a first-time employee, he confessed to having been in love with me from my very first day. He said that if I went out with him, he would transform the office into an associated company with him and me as the only two partners."

Amos felt the blood rushing to his face but held himself in check. "And now what do you intend to do?" he asked.

"I was waiting to talk to you to ask your advice, to hear what you think," she said.

Amos replied, "There's nothing to think about! On Monday you'll go to work and quit."

"I thought of that at first, but it's just that I'd be sorry because it's my first job and I like it, I'm earning money—" She broke off and she began to cry. Amos took her in his arms, hugged her tightly, and tried to console her, without, however, changing his mind: Marica *had* to leave that job. She would find a better one.

"People of goodwill always finds something to do, and you are not lacking in goodwill, my love. Why are you so sad?"

Marica eventually promised to do as Amos had suggested. She dried her eyes and quickly they went to Amos's house; she left only after he was calm and serene again. Returning to her house, she felt sorry that she had to quit her job. Deep down, the prospect of being a partner and director of a firm—of passing so easily from one shore to the other—had tickled her fancy and flattered her vanity; yet her love for Amos was still strong, not to mention the fact that marrying him would have been anything but disadvantageous . . .

Marica's story had ended Amos's feeling of security, and from that moment on he adopted an attitude that one should never hold with one's partner: he started prying into her private life, and if they weren't together for even one day, he would besiege her with questions about what she had done, whom she had met, and so on. Questions that Marica found unacceptable, and rightfully so.

❧❧❧

After his successful completion of the exam in commercial law, Amos decided to take a brief vacation with a friend from law school at his parents' apartment at the Lido di Camaiore. He said good-bye to everyone and left for the beach, where he stayed until the beginning of the next week. When he returned home he found an unpleasant surprise: over the weekend, Marica had met a boy who had invited her to go dancing; and seeing that her boyfriend had left her alone, she had accepted. Not only that, but she had fallen in love with her new friend and therefore had no intention of continuing her relationship with Amos.

Abandoned, Amos took stock of the situation and didn't make a scene, but he suffered a great deal and it was a long time before he again felt any sense of peace.

19

THERE BEGAN ONE of the saddest periods in Amos's life. He was silent and became a bit of a hypochondriac; he rarely went out with his friends, and when he did he spoke only of his ex-girlfriend and his hopes of getting her back: in short, he bored his friends by always repeating the same words.

He missed Marica. With her he felt comfortable; she was capable of helping him with an ease that no one else had. Furthermore, his studies were not going well, and even in his relationship with music he was undergoing a kind of crisis.

Several years earlier, during his adolescence, his voice had changed, preventing him from singing for a few months; when he tried to recover his voice, he thought that he would have to quit singing opera. He could, more or less, sing some modern songs, in addition to Adriano's compositions. He thought he had lost the one thing that he felt distinguished him from everyone else. His best quality.

To complicate the picture, his allergies, from which he had always suffered, became worse, above all in the springtime but also during other times of the year. A little dust was enough to make him immediately start sneezing and for his eyes to water, and he suffered from unbearable rashes. Nothing was able to alleviate the irritation. He underwent a series of tests which confirmed that he was allergic to certain plants, cats, and various types of pollen. The doctor also suggested that he stay away from horses to avoid contact with hay. But renouncing horseback riding for Amos meant renouncing his masculine and slightly wild lifestyle, which was one of the things he held dearest.

All these things, which happened over a period of time but which had now all come to a head, made him suffer and above all disoriented him. Difficulties and pain: was this, perhaps, his destiny? At times he felt defeated, despondent, finished, but at other times not much was necessary to lift his spirits: a kind word, a nice meal, an idea, and his optimism and exuberance reappeared; but then his mood would change and he would say to himself that sooner or later life rewards those who love her with all their strength; he would then set himself goals, and vow not to rest until he had reached them.

Two of Amos's great passions, singing and horses, were, or seemed to be, now impossible. This was too much, simply too much: before giving up he had to leave no stone unturned. He kept a diary. Some lines that he wrote at the time allow for an understanding of his state of mind:

I had dreams that I jealously guarded in the depths of my heart, and even those have been dashed against the wall of reality; they have shattered into a thousand pieces, but I have bent down, gathered them up, and now, with infinite patience, I put them back together. I will give them wings so that they may learn to fly and little by little rise to the heavens, perhaps even to overcome that wall and to migrate there where dreams come true, first in the shape of ideas and then as concrete facts . . .

With the help of a pharmacist and some medication, Amos continued to go horseback riding; indeed, he now went more often than ever before, almost maniacally. He returned to studying piano, and also became interested in electronic music. He purchased an electronic drum kit. He even looked for a place that would hire him as a pianist. It was a way of passing time between one exam and the next, to earn his first paycheck, and to find some new places and meet new friends. But above all, Amos decided that he could not abandon music.

One day a small piano bar, the Boccaccio Club, asked him to replace their old piano player. Amos learned some pieces by heart and went to meet the proprietors who were to be his first employers. He quickly realized that he enjoyed the work. He played easily while the patrons drank, chatted, began and ended love affairs. Only a few, a very few, really listened to him. Amos could play and sing whatever he wanted and only rarely did someone request a song. Every once in a while a girl would notice him, lean on the piano and say a few words to him, and show signs of an interest that Amos reveled in. The girls would place their glasses on the piano and, to give themselves an air of sophistication, would light up a cigarette. Amos could sense their gestures. The fact that they smoked annoyed him somewhat, but he said nothing, and when he found them kind and nice, he didn't even notice their smoking.

His work ended very late. When he was finished, he would get up from the bench with aching wrists and a painful back, but happy and satisfied. As he usually wasn't sleepy, he would go into the restaurant with some friends, order some pasta, wine, and to finish, some coffee. Sometimes he went into one of the small adjoining rooms where the owners, along with friends and clients, gambled, and he enjoyed following the bets, which often reached incredible amounts. He even made some small bets himself, and would often go home at daybreak. He had time for two or three hours' sleep and then Ettore would come to read or go through a textbook with him. Dead tired, Amos would promise to himself that in the future he would come home early; but the next evening, after work, he wouldn't be sleepy and would change his mind.

Things went on this way pretty much for a year until the day of his graduation from law school.

On Sunday, the only day he could sleep in, Amos usually stayed in bed until early afternoon, even skipping lunch. Then he would go to Poggioncino to visit the horses he had grown to love so much. If the weather permitted, he would saddle the mare and ride through the countryside. One day during one of those rides, near the old mill, a voice called to him. He pulled on the reins and the horse stopped, twitched her ears, and listened, as did the rider. The voice belonged to a girl.

"My name is Gaia," she said. "I live here, but you don't know me because we've never spoken. I called you because I'm crazy about horses and would love to ride with you!"

Amos jumped to the ground, shook hands with Gaia, who seemed very young to him, and asked her if she would like to ride bareback with him. She said yes, and began to laugh.

"Wait for me here," said Amos, "I'll go drop off the saddle and return. I'll be right back," He galloped off at full speed, showing off his abilities as a rider. After only a few minutes he returned. Gaia was waiting for him. Without dismounting from the horse, Amos slid back a bit. Following his instructions, the girl nimbly grabbed the mane, took a leap, and was on the horse's back. Amos helped her into a safe position, well forward, between the shoulders of the horse; then he delicately touched the animal with his heels, and the mare began to move slowly, as if afraid to unsaddle the two young riders. Passing the old mill, which had been converted into a hen-house, they took a path that ran alongside the forest and led to an abandoned farmhouse, owned by the Bardi family. Amos rode with confidence, but the slender feminine body that was between his arms, the windblown hair that tickled his face, and the happy voice speaking to him were severely distracting him. He felt tenderness, along with a warmth that soon became a burning flame that confused his mind and demolished his willpower.

When they reached the isolated farmhouse Amos proposed to

the girl that they allow the horse to rest awhile. They jumped to the ground and Amos pulled a cord from his raincoat, removed the harness from the animal, attached the snap hook of the cord to the central ring of the halter, and tied the other end to a bell walled into the facade; then he invited Gaia to follow him up the exterior stone steps to the second floor of that abandoned cottage. Gaia followed him; she didn't seem to be embarrassed at all. They entered a large empty room, and Amos took off his raincoat, laid it on the floor, and invited the girl to sit next to him.

First they talked about horses, then the conversation became more general. Amos caressed her hair and occasionally, with the back of his hand, he brushed her warm cheeks; then he took her hand and squeezed it between his hands; finally, all of a sudden, he embraced her, clasping her resolutely and kissing her.

When Amos came to, he couldn't figure out how much time had gone by. He jumped up, remembering the horse, held only by an old cord: excusing himself, he ran down to the yard. The horse was gone. To have left her in such a way was an irresponsible act; the animal could have crossed the main street and been hit by a car or motorcyclist. The snap hook was still intact; with a mighty pull, the beast must have broken the ring of the halter; even if he found it, it would be difficult to put the bit back in place. He knew something must have alarmed her to make her take off so suddenly.

"Zara! *Zaraaa!*" He yelled the horse's name, though he knew full well that since she wasn't particularly obedient, she would never come running back. Amos knew that startled horses usually galloped crazily back to their stalls, where they hoped to find oats and rest. He clasped his hands and offered a prayer to the good Lord, who until that moment Amos had forgotten—and perhaps offended. He then called for Gaia. She was blissfully unaware, as only a fifteen-year-old could be. Her attitude irritated Amos.

"We must run home," he said to her; he grabbed her hand and quickly dragged her away.

At the old mill, Amos called the proprietors. The woman came out breathlessly and told them how she had seen the horse passing there at a gallop: "She must have seen something on the road, maybe a snake, or who knows what, because she stopped here for a moment and then, terror-struck, wheeled back toward the field behind the house. My husband tried to grab her, but as soon as he got near her, she ran off. She has a broken halter. We hope you find her!"

Amos ran with Gaia toward the field. Zara was no longer there. They found her not far away: she was eating peacefully from a bucket filled with grain for the chickens.

Cautiously Amos approached and Zara raised her head and looked at him, uncertain as to whether she should flee or stay; then she nosed the pail again. Amos circled her neck with his arms and calmly managed to pass the reins over her head. Then, with some difficulty, he inserted the bit.

That night at dinner, Amos filled his parents in on what had happened that day. He enjoyed recounting the tale, even though he knew very well that he would be reprimanded for the risks he had taken, not only in tying the horse to a bell, but also and above all for having a young girl climb on the horse and riding too fast with her; they could have fallen and hurt themselves. And, of course, someone might have seen them as they went to the house in the forest—a deserted farmhouse—spied on them, and blurted the information to Gaia's father.

His parents went on and on castigating him, but Amos didn't mind letting the cat out of the bag; for an extroverted character like his it was difficult to keep secrets, and it was a good opportunity to talk about Gaia, who by now was in his heart and had begun to fill the void left by Marica.

The next day Amos saddled Zara again and rode toward his new friend's house. He found her waiting for him as if they had made a date. She greeted him with the eagerness of a little girl and the mischievousness of an adult.

"I knew you'd come," she said, smiling.

Amos pretended to be offended. "If you don't like it I can easily turn around and go back."

"I wouldn't be here waiting for you if I didn't like it," she replied promptly.

Amos continued the little flirtation. "Maybe you're only here because you like horses," he said.

"No," Gaia said. Amos liked the girl's quick spirit.

"Okay, then today no ride. I will go home and unsaddle Zara and wait for you there, if you want."

He prodded the horse into a gallop and Gaia followed him on her motorbike; she helped him take off and put away the harness and to wipe the sweat off Zara; then she walked the horse into the stall and brought her a good serving of oats. She was pleased and smiling; with her arms at her sides, she stopped in front of Amos. He drew her to him and embraced her, overcome by a sudden happiness. But then he detached himself from her and made his way to the nearby well, with the expression of one who has a doubt to clear up.

Why does all this make me so happy? he asked himself, and sat down on the parapet. It was Gaia, coming to his side, who provided the answer. I wasn't born to be alone, he thought; life is so much more easy and pleasurable when it is shared with someone else! He felt a real sense of gratification and well-being.

Gaia was different from his classmates, different from the girls Amos met at the university or the parties he was invited to. She had a unique way of dressing and of carrying herself, of expressing herself: in short, her whole way of being was different. It was a way of life that he himself felt distant from; and yet her spontaneity, her almost animal naturalness, her youthful freshness, her character, which was usually calm but at times became impetuous, generous, and strong-willed, made it fun and surprising to be in her company. Even though she attended the upper school in the city, there was no trace in her of the customs and manners of the city, no attempt—either awkward or successful—

to assimilate the language and habits of the city. She remained a wildflower, a stray dog, a bird of the air, a free and indomitable spirit, close to the spirit of nature, free from conformism and pretentiousness. That's why she loved horses, with which she spoke the silent language of the body and instincts, and that's why she had felt attracted to Amos and had loved him without asking anything from him and without asking anything for herself. Liberated from the shackles of convention, she gave free rein only to that which sprang from her heart.

Amos quickly got to know her: he loved the joy that Gaia was able to give him so much better than anyone else, but at the same time his inability to pin her down, to constrain her personality, bothered him. He tried to get her to accept the idea of going out with him, to let him know that she was wholly and only his, but there was nothing to be done: she arrived and departed every day as if each encounter might be their last. Amos had no assurances. He would have preferred a woman in love, jealous, faithful, morbidly attached to him. In a word, he wished for a Tosca. What he seemed to have instead was a Carmen.

One day he didn't see her. Gaia had failed to keep their afternoon appointment. She stopped by the next day to greet him but didn't stay long. After that, Amos didn't see her for some months, nor did he try to find her, having learned from Sergio that she was seeing another boy from town.

Amos was once again without a girlfriend with whom he could spend time. He went back to seeing his friends, who all had girlfriends. He buried himself in books but couldn't find the necessary concentration. Not even Ettore's joking managed to shake him out of his misery. He took difficult exams, like the ones in civil procedure, in constitutional law, and above all in commercial law, which caused him to suffer more than the others. He simply could not understand such concepts as profit and loss or discounts in commercial law. Ettore, to whom they seemed very clear, tried to understand why Amos remained bewildered and at a loss before those ideas, which seemed to him at that time to be unexplainable contortions of the mind.

"There are minds that are capable of autosuggestion to the point of believing that the easiest things in this world are difficult," he said to Amos. "You know you are preparing for a university exam and imagine that this involves some very complicated ideas. Any store clerk is capable of understanding balance sheets and budgets. You, instead, flounder about and fail to understand."

Eventually, Amos saw Marica again, learned from her that she was once again free, and invited her to his house: Marica accepted and the two teenagers got back together. Amos found he was still in love with her, and his desire had been increased by having lost her for some time. As if nothing had happened between them, they began to see each other every day, and this distracted Amos from his studies just as he was preparing to take one of the most important exams: that in penal law. It was the next-to-last one; if it went well, he would quickly prepare for the exam in penal procedure, and then he would concentrate on his thesis.

Marica, though, was a complication: he could not forget her even during the hours of study. He decided therefore to try taking the exam; but things went poorly. After only two questions, which he answered only partially, the professor asked him to come back at a later date when he was better prepared. Amos got up in disbelief from his chair. It was the first time that he had been sent from the examining hall without even being given a grade. He felt humiliated and discouraged. As soon as he arrived home he called Ettore with the news. Ettore did not seem overly perturbed: he calmly said that he would arrive at the usual time the next day.

A few months later Amos passed the exam in penal law, and gripped by a frenzy, he immersed himself in the textbook for penal procedure. The last exam! He could hardly believe it. Penal procedure presented difficulties solely in terms of memorization. Amos quickly completed the preparation and presented himself, fairly sure that he would pass. He answered the questions well and the professor wrote down his grade and sent him on his way with a good-natured smile.

Amos jumped up and quickly left the hall. When he was outside he stopped in the center of the courtyard of the Sapienza: he had finally cut through all that red tape. There's no time like the present, he thought to himself, and made his way toward the office of the professor of philosophy of law; he had already asked that this professor act as his thesis adviser. He soon found him. Amos sat down, and half an hour later, when he left, the title of his thesis had been decided: *History and Natural Law in Montesquieu.*

Amos was so impatient to complete his law degree that he didn't even take a day off: the next day he was already at work with Ettore, who seemed full of enthusiasm. But after the initial attempts, both of them realized how difficult it was to write something original on a subject on which everything had already been said. Amos became so discouraged that it even crossed his mind to find someone to write his thesis for him, but immediately he was ashamed of the thought, which would have—or so it seemed to him—made his entire university career a waste of time. He thought about leaving for Paris and researching some rare text, or perhaps just in search of new stimuli and ideas. So he paid a spur-of-the-moment visit to Dr. Della Robbia, whom he had not seen in some time. He remembered that in their conversations, Dr. Della Robbia often referred to the French Illuminists (Enlightenment philosophers) in general, and to Montesquieu in particular. Maybe he had something to suggest. And in fact in his library, Amos found essays that he had not yet seen and would not have been able to find elsewhere. He returned home radiant and full of good intentions. Writing the thesis and correcting it was a very long and laborious process: every argument, every sentence, was discussed with Ettore, with whom he had to reach some agreement before the definitive draft was made. These discussions seemed very difficult and dull to Amos. The thesis was taking a very long time to complete.

Marica felt neglected. During his free time Amos preferred going to the farm and riding his horse rather than being shut up in the house with her or visiting someplace along the coast. Marica was bored of waiting for him, and she was even more bored with the countryside, from which she had always dreamed of escaping. Amos's love for animals, plants, walks in the open air, along the river or into the hills, were the things that annoyed her the most about him: characteristics she just was not able to change. Marica could not understand why Amos did not feel the need to lose himself among people and why he didn't share her wish to go out, to know other people and be admired. No: he tried everything to get her to share his passions, to interest her in his projects, to infect her with his dreams.

Time passed and Amos's parents began to show signs of impatience to see their son graduate from law school. He, instead, continued undaunted in reading his books, playing his instruments, riding his horses, boring his girlfriend, and coming home late at night to cook for his friends, to empty bottle after bottle of wine in the middle of the night when everyone in the house was sleeping. Only when he felt ready did he go to the professor and fix a date for the defense of the thesis: April 30 of that year. It was the end of January; there were only three months to go.

This news raised the spirits of his parents, but it didn't help Amos's relationship with Marica: something between them just didn't work anymore. Amos knew it, but refused to admit it. Marica had changed in his eyes: she seemed cold and detached. Amos pretended not to notice. The problem with Marica was a problem he preferred to live with, as one lives with a toothache until, in the end, the tooth has to be pulled out. A few days before he was to discuss the thesis, Amos came to hear from a friend that Marica had been seen in Milan with her new employer, in a compromising situation. That news was a blow to his pride and he felt he could not stand for it. Never before had he suffered like this. Alone in his study, he felt hurt and humiliated; for the first time, after so long, tears came to his eyes. He clenched his fists and sought to hold them back, but his efforts were in vain: the tears ran down his face, which he hid in his hands. He sobbed uncontrollably. After a few minutes he calmed down; he was ashamed and full of self-pity, and he decided to go out to the farm. He didn't have a precise idea what he wanted to do, but he felt the need to make some irrational gesture.

It was already late and everyone except his mother was already in bed. Amos slipped on a coat and went out. He breathed deeply the cold air of the late winter and felt a little calmer. He quickly reached the unpaved road that led to Poggioncino, and after a few minutes he was at the farm. He stopped for a moment to catch his breath and then made his way to the horses' stalls. From the window of the first stall a three-year-old colt, whom Amos had just started to ride, looked out and greeted him with a soft snort. Amos stopped, took the horse's head in his hands and began to whisper softly in his ear. His mother, who had heard him leave and had followed him in the car, found him immersed in that bizarre communion. Evidently, something had happened to her son. She climbed out of the car and called to him, but he didn't answer, so she went to join him.

"Leave me alone. Go home," said Amos, without even turning around.

"But what is it? What's happened?"

"Nothing, nothing. Don't worry. Go home."

His mother said nothing more, but she didn't leave. She sat down in silence on the low wall in front of the stalls and patiently waited for her son to talk to her.

"Mama," erupted Amos, "I want to be alone!"

"Why?" pressed his mother.

"Because I was born to be alone."

"That's the first time I've ever heard you say that. In any event, listen: I'm not leaving you here alone without knowing what's happened."

Amos resigned himself and went to the car. His mother followed him and in a few minutes they were home, where his father was waiting for him. He had gotten out of bed when he heard his wife leave with the car.

Amos never found it easy to hide his pain. So, finding himself in the kitchen with his father and mother, he decided to confess: "Marica has been unfaithful. Tomorrow I will be alone again, and it's not easy."

Then he turned, left the room, ran up the stairs, and shut himself in his room. He threw himself on the bed and was quickly overwhelmed by an avalanche of thoughts; they all seemed lacking in meaning, and the future seemed completely without hope. To start all over from the beginning with another girl seemed inconceivable. And yet reason suggested the opposite. He knew very well that grief like this would pass with time and eventually be forgotten. He tried to transfer these convictions from his brain to his heart, but without success; his heart continued to thud violently, and he felt an almost uncontainable desire for Marica spread through his veins; for her young body, which perhaps by now belonged to someone else. Perhaps Marica had laughed at him; perhaps she had given her body to another man, overcome by passion.

Amos didn't know how to escape these upsetting thoughts. He remained awake for almost the entire night, until finally exhaustion overcame him and he fell asleep.

At ten o'clock precisely, Ettore's voice awoke him with a start. Quickly, the pain returned, but Amos got dressed and went downstairs with only one thought: to telephone Marica and ask for an explanation. Within him, anger fought with a hope that his girlfriend would have some explanation to allay his suspicions.

As soon as Ettore left, Amos took the phone and dialed Marica's number. Alarmed by his tone of voice, the girl ran to his house, without even eating, and followed him into his study. They closed the door and Amos quickly vented all the anger and bile that he had been keeping inside; but the poison, mixed with feelings and passion and therefore diluted, did not have any particularly devastating effect on Marica, who had time to think up and organize a line of defense. She had been in Milan with her boss, she admitted, but for work; as for the compromising situation, she was prepared to directly confront her accuser; she had a clear conscience and nothing to fear.

Amos tried to believe her. He wanted her as he had never wanted her before, and she really knew how to play the part of a woman in love. They made love with abandon, and she left him calm and reassured. But when she was gone, Amos had the opportunity to reflect, and he knew that things could not have been as Marica said they were. The truth will out, he thought, and threw himself headfirst into his thesis.

20

❦❦

AS THE SUN ROSE ON APRIL 30, Amos was still awake, intent on putting his thoughts in order and learning the words he had chosen to open the defense of his thesis. When the cock crowed he realized that he wasn't going to sleep that night. So he slowly began to get ready. Noises were coming from his parents' bedroom. He could hear that his mother was getting up. They made their way down to the kitchen almost together. Mrs. Bardi appeared calm, but in truth she was even more excited than her son. Amos drank his coffee before closing himself up in his room to go over his notes; he came to his senses only when he recognized the sound of Ettore's car. Ettore, punctual as usual, had come to pick him up and accompany him to Pisa.

At the school, Amos found Eugenio, his old friend: he was graduating, like Amos, that very day. Amos indicated to Ettore that he wanted to talk to Eugenio, so Ettore went for a walk and left him with his friend, wishing them both good luck. The two friends began walking up and down under the portico of the courtyard.

Eugenio was the first to be called. He was graduating with a thesis in canon law and managed to capture the attention of the examining committee (which was usually rather distracted and bored) with a disquisition on the defects in the idea of consent in matrimony. Some professors intervened with personal observations or specific questions and so the exam went on for some time, allowing Eugenio to make a good impression and graduate with a high grade.

Immediately afterward, it was Amos's turn. The examiners let him speak without interruption, and dismissed him much quicker.

When he was called back into the room, the head of the committee (who was also his thesis adviser) calmly told him that the committee had enjoyed his work and had conferred the degree with a score of 99 out of a possible 110.

It felt so unreal. He had graduated! For a moment Amos feared he would wake up and find it was all a dream. In a daze, he was suddenly surrounded by photographers outside the examining hall. "Doctor, doctor! May we...please, a shot, Doctor!...Fantastic, and now with the caretaker, it will be a marvelous souvenir...let's also take a photograph with your friend, okay, Doctor...?"

Amos, who any other time would have hated such a performance, played along almost happily. Ettore, meanwhile, had returned and, leaning against a column with his cigarette lit, observed the scene at a distance from the photographers and new graduates. When the group dissolved, Amos and Eugenio joined Ettore. There was a brief exchange of witticisms, then they left together to have a celebratory drink at a nearby bar.

❧❦

Amos came home to find a festive atmosphere. His father had decided to take the entire family to dinner at a nearby restaurant. Eugenio and Ettore were also invited, but Ettore declined, saying he wanted to join his wife. "And besides, one always eats too much at these meals and is not well for the rest of the night," and he added with a laugh, "Old people should stay home at night!"

He said good-bye and left. The family was preparing to leave the house when a car stopped in the driveway. It was the florist delivering a bouquet of red roses with a card to Amos. Amos opened the envelope: it was from Marica. A shadow passed over his face; he put the card in his pocket, placed the roses in his mother's arms, and prepared to leave.

That night Amos was unable to get any sleep. I hope my parents are happy now, he thought. They have suffered on my account and have been so worried about my future, even making me anxious, too. I haven't really accomplished anything yet, true, but the law degree represents an important achievement, especially for those who worried about seeing me lost, a man of no consequence in a society full of overachievers . . . they have seen me catch up with the rest, compete head-to-head with the best-trained competitors; earn a position; they have learned to have confidence in me and I will show them that it is not misplaced. There will come a day when they will forget their worries and be proud of their son.

These thoughts made Amos restless. He got out of bed, went downstairs, and sat down at the piano. Everyone was sleeping, but the sound of the piano would not disturb them: he had a habit of playing at that hour and his parents were used to it by now. He opened a window and a spring breeze came in, warm and scented, which to Amos seemed to carry blessed tidings. He breathed deeply, and returned to playing.

The next day Amos received terrible news: Toledo was dead. Toledo was the groom. Amos had learned the art of taming and training horses from him. That extraordinary man, so recently full of life and strength, had been cut down by an incurable disease. Amos was dismayed and his heart filled with pain.

How can such men die? he asked himself. People quickly forget the dead, but I will never forget Toledo, or anything he taught me.

He thought back to those days in the heart of the the countryside, among the horses, riding alongside the groom, who was the salt of the earth and always said what was in his heart. For ten days Amos had gotten up at five in the morning to meet Toledo on the small farm where he broke the horses. It seemed to him that the world without Toledo would be different: men like Toledo really affect the world around them, by the sheer force of their character.

For several hours Amos forgot the events of the previous day, occupied as he was in thinking about his departed friend. He remembered Toledo's voice, laughingly telling someone who had just fallen off a horse, "The earth stops even thunderbolts!" or saying, "It's not that you're afraid, you're just lacking a little courage," to someone who hesitated before climbing into the saddle. But it is natural for men to overcome pain; and with that thought in mind, Amos allowed himself to be persuaded by his friends to go out for dinner with them that night.

After a few glasses of good red wine, Toledo was transformed into a dear memory, forever enshrined in a special place in Amos's heart, where he would be thought of often. In the days that followed, the death of Toledo and the tragedy of the explosion at the nuclear power plant at Chernobyl often invaded his thoughts and disturbed him so much that he decided to return early from his vacation to begin to do something useful. He called Ettore and began preparing for the state bar exam; at the same time he often visited the office of his aunt—the same aunt who years ago had often put him up—and there he had his first experiences as a young and aspiring lawyer.

In his spare time, however, Amos still dedicated himself to music. He wrote and recorded songs that he began to take to record companies, in Milan or Rome, in the hope of convincing a producer to work on one of his projects. He could not help dreaming about becoming a famous singer. The fact that everyone always asked him to sing, and that he loved to sit at the piano or pick up the guitar, *had* to count for something. But the record-company bosses were not interested in his songs, and said his style of singing lacked originality. Amos, of course, argued against those judgments; at times he was even rude and haughty, but he got nowhere. He would return home angry and bitter, and his parents really suffered to see him defeated and humiliated. In the face of such disappointment, Mr. Bardi always repeated the same thing: a single appearance on an important television show was all that was needed for a breakthrough. But the doors of the television studios were completely closed to those who didn't already have a recording contract or were not known to the general public.

In the mornings Amos went to the police station and to court as a young lawyer; in the afternoon he studied or wrote citations and defense briefs; in the evening he would play piano in one of the local establishments, and there he felt most at ease. In short, Amos kept himself busy, and worked with all his strength, but time was passing and he had not yet found the road he wanted to take in life. His parents seemed to worry about him more and more each day.

They continued to get up at seven each morning to go to work so that they could give their son the opportunity to realize his bizarre dreams, and Amos felt guilt, and a sense of dissatisfaction, which only increased with time.

❧❀❧

One morning, hearing the telephone ring, he ran from his study to answer it. It was his friend Luca, who was calling him about a delicate and urgent matter. He wanted to get together, but Amos begged him at least to give him a clue as to what was up. He could sense the other boy's embarrassment when, after much hesitation, he told Amos that he had seen Marica with his own eyes leaving an apartment building in Tirrenia with a man who was holding on to her very tightly.

Blood rushed to Amos's face and he felt weak. He thanked his friend, hung up, and remained immobile. The news had once again devastated him, but this time he wasn't particularly surprised; deep down he harbored no illusions concerning the faithfulness of his girlfriend, but he knew he had to put an end to things quickly.

He dialed Marica's number and, without bothering with pleasantries, told her he knew all about her infidelities and said he was ending things once and for all. Marica did not attempt to defend herself. She asked only to see him one last time, and Amos didn't have the strength to say no.

She arrived soon after. Amos got into her car and together they drove toward Poggioncino. They parked behind the hayloft, and before she even started to speak, Marica burst into tears. Between sobs she asked to be forgiven and said she would be willing to do the same for any indiscretion Amos might commit in the future, but he remained implacable. "How can you even *think* about going out with other men when you were my girl-friend and came to my house and met my family? How could you visit our friends while all the time you were behaving like a—" He stopped, shuddering at the thought of pronouncing that hor-rible word. There was a long pause, then Amos said, "I feel no rancor toward you. I am certainly no better than you. I have also betrayed you; it happened more than once and with more than one person. You see, therefore, that this relationship was bound to fail."

"But I'm ready to forgive whatever you did," she repeated to him. Amos, too, felt a deep sense of pain; but at least at that moment his sense of what was right was stronger than his love for her.

"Let's not talk about it anymore," he said, opening the car door and getting out. "If you like we can take a walk to the river," he suggested, leaning on the hood of the car.

The girl dried her tears, replaced the handkerchief in her bag, and got out of the car. That walk was her last chance. Perhaps this is what she was thinking about while, arm in arm with Amos, she climbed slowly down the path that skirted the forest and led to the lower fields. Fields that soon would be harvested and from which Amos's father would reap several tons of good hay.

At one point they stopped and sat down on the ground. "But at least you'll leave Lupo with me?" asked Marica. She was thinking of the German shepherd puppy that Amos had given her as a gift some months earlier. The puppy, as it was discovered later, had problems with his back paws, due to hip dysplasia; Marica had lavished all her attention on him.

"Can I keep him?" she repeated.

"Of course," Amos answered her; softening, he turned away. "That way you'll remember me when you pet him," he added, and to overcome this momentary weakness, he got up and took in a deep breath.

Marica was sad and thoughtful. All of a sudden she looked up and said: "I'm sure that without me you'll find the right path and all roads will open up to you. You will fulfill your every dream."

Amos smiled sadly: "Now don't exaggerate!"

From her words he had understood that Marica had resigned herself to the inevitable. He knew it was the right moment to bid her farewell. "Well, we should return. I wouldn't want people to look for me and worry," he said.

Marica got up and silently they retraced their steps along the shadowy path, with the forest on their left and the valley, the fields, the meadows, and the River Sterza—almost completely dry—on their right. The rustle of a lizard in the grass attracted Amos's attention; he turned to listen then continued walking, as a strange thought began to take shape in his mind: "These plants will never see us together again, and I don't know why—because of morality or custom. The fact remains that when a woman betrays her man, in many cases he loves her and desires her as never before. And yet he must leave her forever if he doesn't want to lose his self-respect and the esteem of others. And to think that moral laws, human conventions, and traditional customs are born and take root for the benefit of men! Every society creates its own laws; then the demands of progress, or simply change, induce the most intelligent, the most perceptive, the most enterprising to *break* those laws, often paying the price. And this means that slowly but surely, everyone eventually finds normal what had previously been judged to be immoral."

Amos was so immersed in these thoughts that he didn't realize that they had reached Marica's car; only when she opened the door for him did he return to reality.

After a few minutes he found himself in his study, alone. He took down a book from the library: it was a collection of Chopin's études. He opened it, placed it on the music stand of the piano, sat down, and tried to find some peace in the music. He read the Braille score but the notes made no sense musically in his mind, which was occupied with other thoughts. So he got up and started walking up and down. He had confessed his infidelities to Marica. Stunned, he realized that he had never considered them such before. How strange! Either his behavior had to be considered entirely innocent, in which case he had to forgive Marica's behavior as well, or he should have felt as guilty as she. He had often heard it said that when a woman gives herself, she does so for love, while a man is able to separate his emotions from sex. That concept, which he had previously shared, now seemed ridiculous and foolish. He had known and befriended girls who thought and acted exactly like boys. His mind was lost in a sea of ideas from which he could not escape. He felt tired, and with the slowness of an old man he climbed the stairs, shut himself in his room, threw himself on the bed, and fell asleep.

21

AFTER AN HOUR AMOS woke up cold and in a bad mood, went downstairs, and entered the kitchen, where his parents were speaking in low voices. He got the impression that they were talking about him, and this made him worry. He felt a strange annoyance with his parents. He turned and walked into the living room, switched on the stereo, and began walking up and down, listening to the music and ruminating on the idea of leaving home and living on his own.

A man of my age should have his independence, he thought. He must be free to manage his own affairs without being criticized and judged all the time. There's no need to go far away. I could just move to Poggioncino, into one of the two small flats that Father has just finished renovating. The house in front will soon be ready, too...

The house in front was one that his father had begun to renovate so that it would be ready for the day his son got married; but the work was lagging so much that Amos suspected his father of harboring a poorly hidden aversion to the idea of his son marrying Marica. Mr. Bardi had never felt that she was the right girl for his son. He had made it clear once or twice with a few cutting words, but had not returned to the subject; the work on the

141

house, Amos's pressure notwithstanding, was not going forward. Now Amos was forced to recognize his father's farsightedness. On the one hand, this perspicacity wounded and offended him; on the other, it increased his respect for his father and renewed the feeling (until recently denied) that his father could still protect him from life's dangers; infantile feelings that in his moments of darkest distress constituted for Amos something to cling to, a reason for hope.

Taking the opportunity provided by a weekend that the Bardi family had decided to spend at the Lido di Camaiore, Amos told his father that he would no longer stay at home but would be sleeping at Poggioncino, in one of the flats. Mr. Bardi was not particularly happy, but raised no objections, and so Amos was able to carry out his project of living independently. As for Mrs. Bardi, she seconded the initiative, thinking that perhaps it would help her son overcome once and for the emotional issues that made him suffer so, and that had rendered him different from his normal, cheery self. Before leaving for the beach, she cleaned and organized the apartment her son had chosen, supplying some things that were missing and planning on completing the task when she returned.

So began a period of freedom for Amos. He spent the time with Cristiano, a young friend who was just starting out at the university. At night they went to Chianni, where Amos played until midnight. Cristiano helped him set up and take down the instruments and cables; then they ate with the restaurant owners. The meal usually lasted until late, and didn't end until the carafe of wine at the center of the table was completely empty. Often, some other friends joined the group, and sometimes some lively girls. Amos would suggest that they finish the evening at his place, and everyone would go to his flat, which, though tiny, was furnished with everything necessary: a perfectly functioning kitchen, a small bathroom, two small bedrooms with wrought-iron beds. When his friends finally left and Amos got ready for bed, it was already daytime. The men making their way to work in the fields would spot him on the doorstep and ask him why he had gotten up so early; and Amos would respond, laughing, that he had not yet been to bed.

He slept little and often skipped meals. In the afternoon he would saddle up his horses or try to train some friend's or acquaintance's colt: a risky activity and one that everyone advised against but that Amos did not want to give up. The colts allowed Amos to demonstrate his courage and skill. When he mounted one for the first time, there was always a small crowd around the corral to watch the horse-breaking, and Amos, overcoming his fear, tried with all his might to do everything that Toledo had taught him. He felt satisfied and proud of himself. These were his moments of glory. Then he would run home to prepare for the evening—or rather for the night.

Soon his parents began to worry about Amos's health, and about the gossip that was circulating about him. To his mother Amos looked pale and weak. Mrs. Bardi worried that he might contract some disease from the women he slept with; at night she and Mr. Bardi weren't able to sleep thinking that he might be driving around in the car with Cristiano, both of them tired and drunk. But a lucky star shone over Amos and his guardian angel was truly diligent: Amos fell from horses without getting hurt, he led a dissolute life but his health didn't suffer too much from it, he was a single man, yet everyone seemed to love him.

Adriano, in the meantime, had found work as a bank clerk, had gotten married, and had a daughter; even so, every Friday he went to his friend's house and together they composed songs; then they moved to the kitchen and prepared enormous plates of pasta *alla carbonara* (Amos had learned to beat the eggs and prepare the sauce with onions, garlic, and bacon). They had long discussions about life, friendship, and love, and they understood each other so well; they drank the fine wine made by Amos's father and sometimes they lit up a Tuscan cigar. Now Amos liked to smoke them until the very end and he put them out only when he could no longer bear to hold them. He inhaled and quickly exhaled the smoke out of his mouth, but then he inhaled it again through his nose: that inebriating perfume helped him to dismiss any burdens and worries, fears and dissatisfaction. He became happy and talkative, he spoke of himself, his dreams, of those things that prevented him from realizing them—things to do with the injustice of the world and the shameful compromises made by other people, who would stop at nothing to accomplish their own ends. Amos spoke without thinking for a moment of examining his own defects, his laziness, his superficiality.

Adriano listened to him patiently and with understanding, and Amos, who thought him honest, was proud of his respect. The idea had taken root in his mind that the record producers were all obtuse and incapable, while the directors of the television stations were all corrupt servants of power. A career based on the ancient values of honesty, talent, and discipline seemed impossible to him. His state of mind prevented him from realizing the mediocrity and futility of those ideas. If he had stopped to reflect only for a moment, he would have seen that everyone who fails to excel thinks in this way. Only after Adriano had left and he was alone did doubt begin to torment him and his earlier euphoria dissolve. Then Amos would go to bed.

In the morning, after washing his face with cold water as he had always done since the days of boarding school, he would ponder the discussions of the previous evening and would be ashamed at how he had revealed his frustrations, his weaknesses, and the least noble part of his character.

❧❀❧

Ettore still went to see Amos every day, bringing textbooks with him; and those readings were always the catalyst for an animated discussion. Through that difficult time, Ettore continued to be a stable point of reference for Amos. Without being patronizing, Ettore advised Amos every day to be more decisive, not to follow mad dreams and vain hopes; his studies could always turn into a lifetime project and did not preclude the possibility of pursuing an artistic career, if that's what he wanted. To Amos, Ettore's attitude was annoying, but he had to recognize the validity of the argument, even if he felt a rebellion growing in his heart day by day at what seemed to be his destiny. Something told him not to give in, not to lay down arms, not to yield to those who didn't believe in him, to those who laughed at his illusions. He continued to write songs, to rehearse, to mail tapes out left and right, hoping that someone, somewhere, would recognize his talent, but every time he heard the same things: being good is not good enough, one had to be more original, more individual. Amos rebelled, debated, argued; in the meantime, though, he knew that something had to change.

Around that time he met a young classical pianist, and thought about returning to study piano with him. To widen his musical acquaintances could only help him. Carlo—this was the name of the pianist—had declined at first; he thought Amos would not seriously dedicate himself to a course of study that required discipline and sacrifice, but Amos had so insisted that Carlo decided to give it a try.

The two quickly became friends. Their relationship went well beyond the feelings that usually tie a pupil to a teacher. Carlo would sit at the piano and accompany Amos in some aria. At first there were problems: Carlo played in a precise style, almost pedantically so, and Amos sang too freely, but after a while they discovered the pleasure of making music together. Carlo began to grow passionate about opera and soon could accompany Amos in any aria, without hesitation. Able to sight-read extremely well, he would arrange a score on the piano ledge and would play, much to the joy of Amos, who finally was able to test his voice and its interpretive qualities, without being hampered by having to walk back and forth in his room and stopping to change the record on the turntable.

Amos found fresh energy and a new enthusiasm. He bought a cart in which he put all his electronic equipment, attached it to his father's Land Rover, and lugged it along with him to play everywhere: in local nightspots, country festivals, feasts, weddings, hotels, restaurants, even in town squares. His father accompanied him. He would drive, and carry the heavy amplifiers, loudspeakers, and keyboards on his shoulders, and Amos would deal with the wires; everything would be ready in no time. There would be a little time to mop his brow and freshen up, then Amos would begin to play and sing for two, three, or even four hours nonstop. He felt gratified and serene: it seemed as though the performances helped to tame his wild and dissolute life.

❧

One summer evening, together with Cristiano and Mario, a friend from Sardegna whom he had known for some time, Amos went to Boschetto, an open-air nightspot where he loved to play because he could breathe the fresh air and because the company was pleasant. Like every other night, he hurriedly assembled his equipment and got to work. Suddenly, while he was singing, Mario reached toward him and interrupted him cheerily, slapping him on the back. Careful to speak softly so that his voice wouldn't carry into the microphone, he said in Amos's ear: "There are two good-looking girls here who want to meet you!"

In the meantime, the two had reached the steps of the small stage that was set up for the pianist. Mario signaled that they should come up. Shyly they came closer. Mario introduced them to Amos, who, as is often the case in such situations, didn't even get their names. He shook hands with them, said something kind, and promised to take a short break soon and sit down with them. The two girls said good-bye and returned to their seats.

Less than fifteen minutes later Amos was sitting at a table with his two friends and the two girls they had just met. He sensed that Claudia and Elena were really very nice and cheerful, and ascertained that they were both very pretty, wearing summer dresses that showed off their suntans. They confessed to being just seventeen years old; Elena was preparing for her last year in the classical *liceo,* Claudia for her next-to-last year in the scientific school. Amos enjoyed listening to their youthful conversation, their restrained laughter, their clear voices, and occasionally he intervened with a question or comment. He was enjoying himself so much that he didn't realize that he had extended his break longer than usual. The proprietor came to the table, took a chair, and sat down beside them. Amos understood immediately and got up, but the proprietor, with an affable air, asked if Amos didn't want something else to drink before returning to work, and when Amos declined, was so kind as to add, "Play something, but hurry up and take another break and come back to these two. They're worth it."

In the interval between two songs, Mario spoke to him again, but Amos was puzzled: was it really worth spending so much time with two girls of good family, so young and innocent? They certainly wouldn't care for two "old-timers" like Mario and himself, not to mention that Elena's father was a famous lawyer. "We'll end up in jail!" said Amos, laughing.

Mario didn't agree. Amos was really saying this just to say it: in reality he couldn't wait to return and sit at the table with Elena and Claudia. The two young girls attracted him the way a glass of fresh water attracts a man who is parched with thirst.

When he stepped down from the stage, he had to stop at other tables and linger with people who congratulated him and requested their favorite songs. Then the proprietor dragged him to the bar to introduce him to some particularly dear friends. Amos was restless but was forced to stay there, with his usual good manners, conscious that public relations has a great importance, in whatever one's line of work. Meanwhile Mario had questioned his new friends and found that Elena was attracted to Amos: to his voice, but not only that. He got up, ran to his friend, excused the rude interruption, took him by the arm, and when they had walked away a few paces said to him, laughing, with his strong Sardinian accent and ringing voice: "I've always said to you that when it comes to women you know nothing, absolutely nothing! We're not as old as you say . . . I think this could be a lucky night, especially for you."

Amos invited Claudia and Elena to go on a trip to the beach the next day. When the group reached the beach at Cecina, Amos took Elena by the arm and withdrew from the others, speaking to her in a more serious tone than he'd done the night before. He asked her to tell him something about herself, of her character, her dreams; then it was his turn to create a kind of autobiography. He had never felt, as he did at that moment, the need to describe himself honestly, emphasizing his defects and downplaying his virtues. He understood that Elena saw in him a strong and courageous man, and thinking back on his recent past and his wild life, almost felt unworthy of her, because she was so sweet and good. But he also had the feeling that something in him was changing.

The sun burned on their skin. They wet their heads and shoulders, then turned around to find some shade. They lay down on the sand next to each other. Perhaps it was at that moment that they realized that they were no longer two strangers but two beings created to live together: their lips, which searched for each other, joined in a kiss that was a sweet promise for both, irrespective of their different ages, their different life experiences, their different ways of seeing things and judging things. Elena was attracted to Amos's maturity, his confidence, his physical strength;

Amos was touched by her youth, her innocence, her fresh laughter. She didn't try to protect him or mother him but asked rather to be guided, advised, defended, shaped. By her side, for the first time in his life, Amos felt like the man he had always, deep down, wanted to be.

22

❧⁖❧

A FEW DAYS LATER Elena visited Lajatico. Amos was anxious to show her all the places to which his most beautiful memories were attached. He had decided to show her the town even though it was late summer and the afternoon sun was burning, making the air almost unbreathable. They walked around the piazza and entered the bar on the corner of the Via Garibaldi, where they asked for two glasses of cold water. All the clients who were seated at the small tables drinking or playing cards glanced at Elena, whom no one knew or had seen before. To her, it seemed as though everyone had suddenly lowered the tone of their voice and the hubbub of a moment ago had—at least temporarily—been lowered to a whisper. During the journey there, Amos had regaled Elena with tales of the curiosity that reigned in small towns. Struck by the immediate confirmation of this in the bar, she smiled as if to say, "You're right once again."

A little farther on, crossing the Via Garibaldi, they entered a small amusement area, where they found an empty bench in the shade of one of the tall oak trees. They both felt tired and terribly hot, but happy to find themselves together: there, or anywhere else, it would have been the same. After a long silence, Elena turned to Amos: "I want to be with you forever!" she said.

Amos smiled and kissed her. "So then you want to stay with me tonight, preparing something for dinner, and . . ." The afternoon seemed truly too short.

"If only! But what will I say to my parents?"

"We'll think about that later." Amos was excited at the idea of spending the entire night with her. Finally they would be alone, in the great family house. It would be a taste of future happiness.

"Go and buy something," added Amos. "Look, in the piazza there are two grocery stores, you only have to choose which one."

He took out his wallet and gave Elena a 100,000-lire note. Elena paused for a moment, uncertain, then she made up her mind, got up slowly, and left. Left alone, Amos stretched himself out on the bench with one arm under his head, closed his eyes, and lost himself in a dreamy state in which reality and imagination blended together. Following Elena in his mind, he imagined her walking, looking around, exchanging glances with the people; saw her blush, look for the store; then he heard her voice calling him, so he got up and accompanied her to the entrance of the store. "I'll wait for you here," he said, and leaned against the wall with his hands behind his back.

Elena approached the door, but suddenly a girl came running by and bumped into her, without taking any notice of it. Elena had to stop the door from hitting her in the face. Then she pushed it open and entered. She took a few steps and stopped, as if she wanted to organize her thoughts. It must have been the first time that she had gone food shopping without her mother or a friend. Amos was thinking about this, when the girl who had bumped into Elena left the store in a hurry: it was Carla, a student who lived in a village not far away. Amos had had a fling with her that lasted only a few days and had ended a month before. After a few moments the glass doors of the store opened again and out walked another girl with a bagful of groceries. She passed in front of Amos and distractedly said hello. It was Gaia. Then a loud, angry female voice from the store reached Amos: "Excuse me, I put this aside for myself! I'm sorry, but you have to get another one!" That Emilian accent was unmistakable. Was she really there, too?

"She" was a girl Amos had been in love with an entire summer who eventually revealed herself to be so insincere and opportunistic as to deeply disgust and embitter him. What was she doing in Lajatico? Did she want something from him or did she have something against Elena?

While Amos was pondering these questions, the Emiliana girl, too, left the store without noticing him. Thank goodness, thought Amos. He entered the store and was greeted cheerfully by the cashier, who called to Elena: "Look, miss, I think this man is looking for you."

Elena turned and was making her way toward Amos when another voice caused him to start: it was that of Marica, who fleetingly greeted him and left, carrying loads of groceries. How strange, thought Amos. Why are they all here?

Meanwhile Elena came toward him with a package of three very small sausages. "These were the last ones. There was a girl in front of me who bought all the others. These were all that were left, so I bought them. They were the smallest, but who knows? Maybe they're the best, right?"

Amos smiled and tenderly stroked her long hair, which fell to her shoulders. "I'll go look for something else. I won't be long, wait for me here," she said, and made her way to a counter where a thin, short, middle-aged shop assistant with a sickly complexion and nervous gestures was slicing bread and displaying perfect pieces of focaccia and triangles of schiacciata with oil and stuffed with salted prosciutto. Elena asked for the prosciutto and the woman wrapped five or six slices, but when she found him again, Elena seemed almost sad to Amos.

"What's wrong?" he asked.

She replied in a low and sulking voice: "The woman at the counter wrapped up some prosciutto full of fat that the girl ahead of me had refused. But I . . ."

Amos felt himself overflowing with joy and tenderness. He wanted to console her, to tell her that prosciutto with fat was much better, but he wasn't able to.

Where does such sweetness come from? he asked himself. How can I stop myself from contaminating her innocence? I shall marry her and stay close to her, and make her happy to be by my side, and proud of me.

All of a sudden something happened that rudely interrupted his train of thought: a strange heat on his face forced him to wake up, confused because of his sudden sleep and his very strange dream. Elena had returned and, discovering him asleep, had covered his face with her hands as she often did when it seemed to her that Amos was sad. She knew that under her hands his smile would return; she raised her hands to see if he had awoken, then pressed her lips to his. That kiss, which signaled the end of Amos's other sexual escapades, was also the seal of an unspoken—but no less binding—proposal. Randomly mixing together events, sensations, old and recent experiences, painful and pleasurable memories as if they were tarot cards, the dream had brought clarity to Amos's heart and mind. I will marry her, he thought, with the intensity of one who proclaims a judgment, and in his heart he felt happy. That night at dinner, Amos reflected on the dream. Compared with the other girls he had known until then—some of whom had passed before him in the dream like stills from an old film—Elena was surely the truest, the sweetest, and the closest to his ideal of a companion. As if the dream had continued, he embraced Elena and said for the first time: "I love you!"

❦

Some days later, seated on the bench behind his keyboard and surrounded by his many electronic devices and gadgets—which he
constantly substituted with newer and more up-to-date equipment—Amos felt inexplicably sad. That evening his parents and
even Elena had been with him; but the restaurant they had visited
seemed to him to be nothing but a squalid shed and the bad
weather that raged outside put him in a foul mood. But perhaps
there was another reason, more serious and more profound: what
would become of him and any family that he might have if he
didn't find a better and more secure job than the haphazard trade
that he plied, which forced him to wander from one piano bar to
another and gave him neither satisfaction nor reasonable assurances for the future?

These uncertainties, which he seemed also to discern in his
parents, made him gloomy and irritable; when he played he
couldn't wait to finish. Elena, who sat at the table of her future in-
laws and never lost sight of him, realized her boyfriend's unease,
left the table, and came to sit next to him. Amos stopped singing,
and continuing to play on absentmindedly, he began to speak with
her and make plans for the future. Then, almost without realizing
it, he asked her if she was ready to get married. Elena was both surprised and happy. Her joy was uncontainable.

But the more Elena's enthusiasm and joy grew, the more
Amos's doubts grew oppressive; doubts that, of course, had nothing to do with her but with his own capacity to provide for his
new family and make it independent and happy. Elena, it was
true, promised she was ready for any sacrifice, but he didn't want
to run the risk that financial problems and his incapacity to find a
steady and satisfying job would jeopardize their relationship. He
would start a family only when he was certain that he had the
necessary financial as well as emotional resources. To depend on
parental support would have seemed like the worst form of
humiliation.

He spoke with Elena, but she didn't understand, and didn't

want to understand. She was a woman in love both with him and with the idea of matrimony. But Amos's attitude, in some ways justifiable, was the cause of many painful arguments between them.

Eventually fortune would change for Amos and such arguments would no longer be necessary.

23

DESPITE THE WAY HIS DREAMS went up in smoke one after the other, his hopes were revealed as vain, and his efforts came to nothing, Amos continued to strive to achieve his goals. Yet something in him was changing. In the meantime, he had enrolled in a postgrad course with the intention of preparing for the state exam, and during his free time he continued to record songs, to send off tapes, to play and sing in the places where the competition was increasingly fierce and the pay got worse, mainly because of the introduction of the computer and synthesizer, over which the musicians merely had to hum. Amos was perfectly aware that he could no longer depend on such work, he knew that time wasn't on his side. He was no longer twenty years old, and there was no reason for excessive illusions anymore; despite all this, instead of feeling exasperated, defeated, or even seriously worried, a calm serenity and a new energy made him sure of himself, and strengthened him more every day: the idea of doing everything possible, searching with all his own strengths to improve himself through study and daily labor, made him feel at peace with his own conscience.

"After the rain comes the sun," Ettore had told him on many occasions, and there was something inexplicable, indecipherable, on which Amos founded the firm conviction that for him there would soon be a ray of sunlight. He greeted the success of others with sincere admiration, even in the field of music, and he laughed at anyone who tried to be tactful, in case they wounded his artistic ego.

Life seemed simpler and more beautiful. Amos felt lighter and freer, more open-minded, and so many things started to seem clearer to him. Considering his songs more objectively, he became aware that they did lack a certain originality and, probably, even strength. They were the creations of an industrious author, musically and grammatically correct, but nothing more. His singing could be judged pleasant, for the tone and timbre, but in it there were evident tensions, something forced, that in the end didn't leave anyone satisfied, even him. What was to be done?

One day, finished with his job, the piano tuner invited Amos to play. Amos sat down, unwillingly played some scales and some arpeggios, then, after having modulated in C-flat major, he began to play Schubert's "Ave Maria." Fearing the difficulties of the left hand, to which the score entrusts the entire responsibility of the accompaniment, he decided to let his voice follow the line of music around the last chords of the introduction. The tuner leaned his elbows on the end of the piano, preparing himself to listen. At the conclusion of the piece, Amos sprang up off the stool and, smiling, invited the young man to put his tools away and follow him into the kitchen for a cup of coffee.

The tuner seemed deep in thought. Was he perhaps looking for something nice to say about the piece Amos had just played? Amos would have liked to have done away with his embarrassment immediately, but the tuner interrupted him and said, "Forgive my frankness, but I feel it is my duty to tell you that, with your voice, you could go a long way if only you entrusted yourself to a good singing teacher."

Amos was very surprised. For years nobody had spoken to him about studying singing; since he had stopped thinking of a theatrical career, he hadn't even taken it into consideration. Now this unexpected advice, which, to Amos, seemed honest and sincere, made him reflect. "I know an exceptional teacher," continued the tuner, "an elderly retired maestro, who returned recently to his home city of Prato. For his whole life he has worked with the greatest singers of the last fifty years and he now gives private lessons. If you want, I can take you to him, since I have to go and tune his piano."

Amos was silent. "Think about it," the tuner concluded.

Amos walked back and forth in the room, stopped unexpectedly in front of the other man, and said: "If you will have lunch with me, we'll talk about it."

"Okay, that's fine with me," replied the tuner.

❧⸙❧

Some days later Amos sat in the car next to his mother on the way to Prato. It was just before Christmas. They parked in the Piazza Mercatale and walked toward the cathedral. When they were a few steps from the entry of the church, Amos held his mother back by her arm, struck by a sweet melody that he had immediately recognized as the famous adagio of Albinoni. His mother was in a hurry, and feared the cold and the gusts of icy wind that whipped them in the face. Crossing the piazza, they took the Via Magnolfi and after a few steps found the residence of Maestro Bettarini.

They climbed four flights of stairs and rang the bell. A kind woman welcomed them, simply but tastefully dressed; she was the maestro's companion. Later Amos learned that she had once been an opera singer and that now she assisted the maestro during lessons. After the introductions and polite conversation, she showed the guests into the study, a spacious room, with the piano in the center, couches, a beautiful desk submerged under papers, bookshelves bursting with books and scores, and a display shelf on which were placed some knickknacks in bronze and silver: a centaur, a chimera, and other mythological figures to which Amos had never really paid much attention.

When Amos entered the room the maestro rose agilely from an armchair and stretched out a hand; then, with a slight bow of the head, he introduced himself to Mrs. Bardi. He was a tall, thin old man, in whose figure and face the lines of an ancient beauty had not entirely disappeared. Amos briefly explained the reasons for his visit, also briefly mentioning his hopes. The maestro listened to him patiently, then sat at the piano. "What do you want to hear?" he asked.

Amos pretended to reflect for an instant then answered, "The aria from *Tosca*. Is that okay?"

"Which one exactly?" the maestro asked him, smiling kind-heartedly at the insufficiency of the information.

"The second—that is the last," Amos hastened to specify, and the maestro, without even looking for the score, began to play those famous notes, written by Puccini for the clarinet, that everyone knows so well.

Amos sang that aria as best he could; as always, he put everything into it, and after the last chord he leaned on the piano, nervously waiting for the maestro's words. In that brief instant he knew that, for the first time, someone was about to express an honest, competent, and perhaps definitive opinion on his voice. If that opinion was negative, he had decided to put his mind at peace; for someone was finally going to tell him the truth.

The maestro assumed a solemn expression and began to speak in the stately tone that certain men assume when they are about to utter eagerly anticipated judgments or pronouncements or advice. "You have a voice of *gold,* my son!" he said. "But..." And here he paused. "But you do the exact opposite of what you *should* do when singing. Proper study would not only improve your interpretative qualities, but it would really strengthen your voice; in short, it would put you in a whole new league. What I mean, to be frank, is that to the ear of the uninitiated what you do may sound surprising, but to the ear of an expert the defects of your voice are egregious..."

Amos listened attentively. Nobody had ever spoken to him this way before. And after all, he had no choice; what the maestro was trying to say to him was: this way is no good, but the right way could be taught—if only he wanted to learn. I want to! Amos thought to himself.

Mrs. Bardi, who had reached the same conclusion as her son in her own way, quickly settled the matter of remuneration for the lessons, the days and times, convinced as she was that she was doing the right thing for her son. Finally, they said good-bye and left.

In the days that followed, Amos learned for the first time about the proper use of the breath, of support, of the diaphragm, of "spun sounds," of "harvest" of voice, of colors, of ringing, of fixed sounds or vibrating ones, and of a thousand other things that opened up new and vast horizons. But he was in a hurry and the maestro reproached him for wanting to rush things. He spoke of the risks associated with the incorrect use of the voice, as well as from overuse, and from bad choices of repertoire. Little by little he introduced Amos to a world that at once fascinated him, bringing him back in time to the unforgettable feelings he'd had when he first heard opera, and intimidated and frightened him.

Amos felt like a teenager falling in love for the first time. He didn't dare believe in it all; he committed himself with all his strength, but it didn't come naturally at first; it was some time before he succeeded in singing without hunching his shoulders, without extending all the muscles of the neck and holding his head still.

Even when these goals were reached, Amos knew that he had taken only the very first steps, and that the majority of the work still lay ahead of him.

The study of singing imposed a new discipline on Amos. Deciding he would leave nothing to chance, he stopped drinking his father's wine and went on a strict diet, similar to that of athletes, so that, in addition to everything else, he felt better: more energetic and fitter, as much in body as in mind. He still did not make the ultimate sacrifice, which would have been the heaviest for Amos to bear and which for the moment he decided to ignore: that of maintaining absolute silence on the days of his performances; a discipline he had heard about, but had always thought of as one of the many myths concerning the most famous opera singers. Later he would accept even this kind of stricture so as to be certain to have done everything possible for his voice, a voice that, day after day, became the one thing upon which he placed all his hopes for the future. His moods were now tied to his vocal performances; moments of exaltation alternated with moments of mistrust and dismay; when he sang too much, so much as to lose his voice, he was immediately gripped by worry; he was consumed with doubts and in his mind dark fears took shape. Amos had absolutely no intention of joining the throng of the disillusioned, who were not always the innocent victims of their dreams, but sometimes had fallen prey to a dangerous overestimate of their own artistic ability, and who often ended up irreparably ruining their own lives and those of the people close to them. But then Amos's voice, after a period of rest, found its sparkle and elasticity again, and his spirits would return to the stars.

❦

One day, leaving the house on his way to a lesson, he met his father at the door. Amos greeted him and told him, "Father, I am nearly there! This, I promise you, will be my last attempt." But in the car, he started to think about doing a vocational course and to work, even as a masseur, or to get a job, even as a telephone operator, in a bank, or an office, public or private; anything would do, any occupation that gave him some way of living without being anymore of a burden to his parents, on whom he was still ashamed of depending at his age.

But late one evening, Amos received a brief phone call that

reignited all his old hopes: a recording studio in Modena, where some time ago Amos had worked on a project that he himself had conceived and financed, now wanted him to come there to sing, together with a famous Italian artist. It had something to do with a new song: a duet between a tenor and a rock star. The recording Amos was invited to participate in was merely a trial run, but he would be heard by key people in the record industry, and if the project went well, who knows, perhaps Amos would be invited to perform the piece in a concert, finally showing the record-industry executives what he was made of.

The following morning Amos departed early for Modena. With him were his mother, who always accompanied him to things like this, and Pierpaolo, a young friend who for some time had helped Amos in his work at the house, in the modest recording studio. In Modena he was welcomed kindly and shown into a small office. Amos did not feel nervous; everyone around was rushing and speaking animatedly about the work that was going on there, in the heart of the recording studio, where some of the most important musicians in the world, directed by one of the artists most loved by the public, were making an album that would surely be an international hit. Amos found himself caught up in that strange atmosphere, in which everything seemed secret and marvelous. In order to appear active and full of enthusiasm, he asked the first person he came across for the score of the piece, to be able to study it well before going in front of the microphone. He began to feel a little nervous, but happy. It almost seemed as though he was living a dream.

The boy to whom he had turned smiled at him kindly. "I don't believe that there is a score," he said, "but don't worry, soon he'll be here in person and he will teach it to you."

To tell the truth, Amos was a little bit stunned, but he didn't have either the time or the inclination to think too much at the time; meanwhile, someone brought him some coffee and around the table on which it was served a vivacious discussion began. Mrs.

Bardi urged everybody to stay calm, but it was clear that she was the most anxious and excited of all; she who had always believed in the unique qualities of her child more than anyone else, and who moved mountains to help him realize his dreams, she who more than anyone else had suffered for his failures, for the time that had passed so fruitlessly for Amos, she now urged calm without being an example of calm to anyone.

Suddenly someone knocked on the door. It swung open and a masculine voice with a markedly Emilian accent announced, with a certain solemnity, "He's arriving!"

Behind him Amos heard some footsteps. The young man who was at the door moved, and three or four people came in. Zucchero, the best known and loved Italian artist in the whole world, had entered the room.

❧❧

Pierpaolo gripped Amos's arm, whispering: "We did it!"

On the return trip, Amos and his companions dreamed about what might be the most thrilling results of that unusual experience. Amos didn't really believe anything of what he himself said, or what he heard, but he pretended to believe everything, or rather he had to force himself to believe, because until that moment there had been so many disappointments and frustrations. He couldn't wait to arrive home and to tell everything to his father, who was so taciturn and introverted, who held everything inside of himself, and who would have given everything—Amos was sure of it—to help realize his son's dreams.

For some days Amos heard nothing about his test, and he made a huge effort to stay calm and serene and to not expect anything special. But in reality, with every day that passed, his anxiety became more and more evident. Was it possible that nobody had noticed him, even on that occasion? But one afternoon, while he was putting on a bathrobe after a warm shower, he was startled to hear the telephone ring. He stopped to listen and heard the voice of his dear old grandmother, who, with the uncertain air of those who are not sure they have heard something properly, said: "I'll get him immediately, wait a moment!" Then he heard her call his name. Amos raced to the telephone. It was a voice that he had never heard before, the voice of a man with an unequivocally Bolognese accent, who courteously introduced himself. "My name is Michele," he said, without being more precise, in the conviction—correct, to tell the truth—of already being known to Amos, who indeed had heard a great deal about him in the last few days. Then, with a haste that Amos couldn't understand, the man at the other end of the line asked him, "I wanted to know, and it is very important that you tell me the truth, if you are absolutely free from any contracts." Amos quickly answered yes. "Then," continued Michele, "I recommend that you don't sign any kind of contract before we meet. Your luck has turned, Amos!"

Amos immediately wanted to know more, and he tried repeatedly to interrupt the kind voice that spoke to him all the way from Philadelphia, way beyond the ocean. Without allowing Amos to interrupt, that voice, which Amos by now would have recognized among a thousand, explained that he had had a meeting with the most famous tenor of our time: the maestro Pavarotti, who for Amos, as for many opera lovers, was a living legend. The maestro, having listened with interest to the voice of Amos, had made some extremely positive comments; indeed, Michele continued, he had not initially believed the story that Amos was a simple unknown piano player in a piano bar who worked in the provinces; he was almost angry with Michele, thinking he was making fun of him; for the maestro could recognize a good tenor from an ordinary voice better than anyone else.

Michele also said other things, but Amos didn't even hear them. At the end of the conversation he warmly thanked him, said good-bye, then, with his heart in his throat, he raced to give his parents the good news. Running downstairs, he entered the kitchen, but found nobody, so he went out into the garden and there found his mother with Elena, quietly working. He told them everything, gripped by a happiness that he couldn't contain. Desperate to share his joy, he said to Elena, "If this really happens then you can begin to think of a date for our wedding!"

At those words the two women, who until that moment had continued to work and had listened only distractedly to most of what Amos had said, stopped. Slowly both were gripped by different feelings and worries. His mother asked him precise questions about his telephone conversation with Michele, whose name had been spoken so often in the last few days in the Bardi house; a man on whom, in Mrs. Bardi's mind, Amos's entire future in the field of music might depend. Elena listened to their conversation lost in thought, then timidly joined the discussion to ask what would happen next, before, with great delicacy, she asked Amos when he thought would be the best time next year for their wedding.

Amos remained vague. Suddenly he felt like a rider who has just released the reins of his horse to leave it free, in its most natural condition, to jump a hurdle. Amos knew the danger of going back on his decision, but like an insecure rider, he wasn't sure he now had the courage to spur the horse on, with his heels, with his voice, with his whole body and mind as well.

24

❧❧❧

THE NEXT FEW MONTHS were frantically busy, what with the preparations for the wedding and readying the old family farmhouse, in which the newlyweds would live. In the meantime, Amos was busy with his singing lessons, piano lessons, and with trying to reach Michele and firm up an agreement that would constitute the beginning of his career.

But Michele was unreachable. Like an eel he managed to elude Amos every time he thought he had tracked him down. If Amos asked for him at the office, the secretary said Michele was in a meeting; if he tried to call him on his mobile phone, Michele might answer, but invariably the line was disconnected or Michele would say he was busy and promise to call back within five minutes; Amos would anxiously wait for the call the whole afternoon before, dejected, he would try to find some plausible excuse for Michele, something that was difficult to do since Amos knew nothing about the way in which a showbiz manager worked. For Amos it was a difficult time, but at least he had a concrete hope to cling to.

The day of the wedding was fast approaching, and Amos grew increasingly worried about how he would provide for his new family. He therefore agreed to sing at a concert, organized expressly for him in a small but delightful theater in a town near his home. Carlo was to accompany him at the piano, and it would be the first real solo operatic concert for Amos: he understood the risk and his teacher had cautioned strongly against it, but Amos felt the need to test himself, to give, so to speak, some meaning and direction to his life.

When Amos found himself in the dressing room, he felt a sense of panic for the first time. He would have liked to flee, to feign illness or perhaps even really fall ill, to somehow get out of performing. But by now everything was ready, and the small theater was full, packed with music fans from neighboring areas, always thirsty for good tenor voices, so rare in our time.

Amos therefore took a deep breath and decided to do it. He sang—or more correctly yelled—with all the voice he had, so that by the end of the concert he felt almost mute. But he gave it his all, and the ordeal finally came to an end. He returned to the dressing room and sat down, ignorant of what was to come; a painful experience which, thinking about it later, he knew he would have to get used to.

Someone knocked on the door. Carlo, who was with him, went to answer, and immediately the small room was filled with people. Someone simply shook his hand and left; others seemed to be arguing with one another. A middle-aged, surly fellow approached Amos and asked, "How do you think you did?"

The sarcastic tone of the question suggested to Amos a prudent reply. "That's not up to me to judge," he replied. "It's up to those who sat in the hall and listened!"

The man patted him on the back and said, "Study long and hard before you sing in public again, or you'll ruin your career!"

An expression of pain and humiliation crossed Amos's face, but he managed to respond spiritedly, "I'll follow your advice."

Then, in the confusion of his thoughts and his feelings, he heard a voice that said, "Yet the timbre is very beautiful!" It was the president of an association of music lovers from a nearby town.

Had he just wanted to say some word of consolation, or was he expressing his true opinion? Amos gave himself no peace.

Now doubts were assailing him again and he felt like a dog beaten by his own master. Back to the drawing board, he thought on the way home. It seemed necessary to begin at the beginning once again. That small step acted as a warning: the path that he wished to take would be neither easy nor happy, but incredibly difficult, bristling with traps, delusions, with inextricable tangles of self-interest and commerciality, many motivations all constantly in conflict with each other . . .

Amos left that painful experience behind and the next day began work again. The maestro Bettarini strongly reproved him, threatening even to stop teaching him if Amos made a similar error. But Amos promised to be more prudent in the future.

In the meantime, he continued his meetings with Carlo, during which he improved his music and voice. Carlo, slightly younger than Amos, loved his work and above all loved music, in which he was indisputably gifted. He had become attached to Amos, and with the passage of time they discovered that besides music, they had many things in common: they both loved good food and good wine, sports, and good company, while neither smoked or gambled, and neither was tempted by the false promises of drugs. They loved life and lived it to the fullest. If what existed between Carlo and Amos was not yet a true friendship, it was at least what could be called a rare form of affinity. They understood each other well and were always in complete agreement, without having to make, as they say, a virtue out of necessity; time would show them how true is the proverb "he who finds a friend finds a treasure."

Thanks to Carlo's patience, Amos quickly made progress with the piano above and beyond their most optimistic predictions. He studied with such determination that he surprised even himself, unaware that his determination stemmed from an unconscious desperation mixed with anger; it is the same feeling that certain athletes have when, in sight of the finishing line, they become aware that their closest competitor has the advantage, and so they fear defeat, which suddenly appears inevitable. But in his studio Amos felt a sense of satisfaction and calm; although he felt mentally and physically tired, he seemed to be at peace with his own conscience. Ettore encouraged him, sending him a message of approval every once in a while, of which Amos was particularly proud. But in the meantime, time was passing and the day of the wedding was near at hand.

In agreement with Elena, Amos had decided that the religious ceremony would take place in the church of Lajatico; then they would celebrate with friends and relatives in the great dining room of the Bardi house. From the beginning Amos had insisted on a simple celebration, not too expensive, but day after day the list of guests inevitably became longer and longer. Even though Amos had initially tried to put off the great day, now that the die was cast he wanted all his friends and family near him. He couldn't explain it precisely but couldn't resist the temptation of adding a name or two to the list now and then.

Meanwhile, occasional calls came from the studio in which he had recorded the song with Zucchero, that place in which all his hopes had been rekindled. The calls left Amos in suspense: first, news came that Pavarotti had refused to sing a piece of popular music and recommended Amos in his place; then it seemed he had changed his mind. In the end the maestro accepted. For Amos, therefore, there was nothing to do but hope that he could take his place next to Zucchero in one of his concerts, something the maestro surely wouldn't do. Amos was deeply saddened, yet who knew if this umpteenth disappointment would somehow reveal itself to be a really lucky break! The fact of singing a melody that had become famous thanks to the interpretation of an artist as important as Pavarotti, the most celebrated tenor of our time, the most charismatic figure in the world of opera, would surely provoke comment and interest from which he could only gain. This idea didn't completely console him, but it lessened his pain somewhat.

It's obvious that this is how things must be, he thought to himself. Meanwhile, a passage from Dante came back to him: "Our path has been willed from above, and one can do only what He has willed; ask no more."

One morning Amos left for Bologna with his father in the hopes of meeting Michele. He had decided to wait for him at the entrance of his office until he agreed to grant Amos a minute of his precious time. When they got there a secretary brought them in and greeted them kindly: Michele, unbelievably, was there, shut in his office, busy with a very important meeting. Surely he would see them.

Amos waited patiently. He was so nervous that the hour or more that they waited seemed like a minute. All of a sudden he heard a door open and Michele came toward him.

"I can talk to you, at long last!" said Amos, smiling happily.

"We are always incredibly busy, especially right now, with the release of Zucchero's new album," answered Michele. "But don't worry, we always find time for other projects as well; I'll do everything possible to send you on tour. Unfortunately now I have to run to the airport because I'm already late."

Michele glanced at his watch, then took Amos's hand and, shaking it, added: "It was a pleasure to finally meet you. I'm sure we will see each other again soon." He also shook Mr. Bardi's hand, who hadn't even had time to say a single word. "Excuse me!" he said again, and pulling on a raincoat that was hanging on a coatrack, he quickly ran down the stairs.

Amos and his father remained immobile, almost in disbelief. So many miles, an entire day; and still nothing resolved? Was it really true? Could *nothing* be done? There was nothing for it but to say good-bye to the secretaries and leave, defeat written all over their faces. On the way home they spoke little, each sunk in his own thoughts.

Amos thought of Elena, who was waiting for him at home; she didn't care about the outcome of the trip, Michele's promises, or the indifference of the record-company executives, because she accepted Amos just as he was. Soon they were scheduled to begin a series of meetings concerning the wedding with Don Carlo, the parish priest of Lajatico; and as one thought drives out another, suddenly Amos found himself thinking about his imminent wedding. His preoccupation gave rise to new worries, a subtle anxiety, almost a pain.

Elena believed in God, but her father had instilled in her an anticlericalism and an antipathy for organized religion. While she certainly didn't try to lecture others about it, Amos was aware of it. During their engagement Amos had taken part in many discussions at Elena's house, in all of which each respected the other's position, but each one more animated and heated than the last. Thinking it over now, Amos knew that he had not managed to alter his fiancée's beliefs at all. To Amos it was the only thing he'd change about her, if he could; the only flaw in the absolute devotion that Elena had demonstrated toward him from their very first meeting. How can I make her understand the necessity, the importance, the *joy* of marrying reason to faith? he wondered. And if she aligns herself to the most rational minds, the most refined intellects of all humanity, how can they waste their God-given intelligence in trying to demonstrate the supposed illogicality of religious people and the futility of religious functions, and by laughing at the credulity of the faithful, instead of using their intellect in a humble way, for the good of all, and professing that poverty of spirit of which Jesus preached during the Sermon of the Mount? Elena is a simple girl, ten times—no, one hundred times better than myself! I am, I know, a man without virtues; I follow virtue with all my strength, but I never reach it, because my strength is too little; and she torments herself for her own incapacity to be what she wants to be. Maybe that's the reason why I can't persuade her.

Amos was so immersed in his thoughts that he didn't even realize he had arrived home. He felt so exasperated that instead of sitting down to the table for dinner, he phoned Adriano. "I just got back," he said, "and I want to talk to you. Can you come over?"

Adriano jumped into his car and in little more than half an hour had arrived. Amos told him about what had happened at the concert, finding it painful and tedious to have to tell his friend about yet another failure; he lingered, though, on the thoughts that had disturbed him during the trip home.

Amos began walking up and down the living room, talking as if to himself, seized by a feverish agitation. Adriano sat on a sofa and listened patiently. "In a few days I will lead a woman who loves me to the altar," Amos said. "We are in agreement, but in church she will sit at my side as if she was at the theater, not unlike the very first time I took her to the opera; she will listen to the priest distractedly, she will make the sign of the cross, she will recite the Apostle's Creed and the Our Father, she may even receive Communion, without, however, being convinced of the Eucharistic mystery; and she will do all this for me, just to make me happy, while I am assailed by doubts, and overwhelmed by confusion, and I no longer know how to tell right from wrong!" He paused. Adriano was silent; he was searching for some word of comfort. "Elena does not deny the existence of God," Amos continued. "Perhaps in her own way she is even searching for Him. Perhaps she is closer to Him than me . . ." Then, sitting next to Adriano, he smiled resolutely, and added: "Oh, let God's will be done! I suppose that's all there is to say."

When the Bardi family arrived home, Amos and Adriano left the living room for the kitchen and closed the door behind them so as not to disturb the others. Forgetting his earlier bad mood, Amos became again the cook that he sometimes loved to be, and soon served up a big dish of pasta *alla carbonara*. He opened a bottle of red wine, and between one glass and another, the discussion grew easier and more animated.

When Adriano left it was late. Amos went to his bedroom, undressed quickly, and lay down in bed, completely immersed in his thoughts. There was something missing from his life, something that made him unsatisfied; something that had nothing to do with his failures in work. It was an undefinable sense of spiritual confusion that bewildered him, a lack of answers to any of his existential problems.

Life passes, Amos thought in the silence of his room, one day after another slips away without leaving you the time to grasp its meaning, without the possibility of appeal, just like that, with no vantage point from which you can judge it, to love it, or condemn it, to be suffocated by remorse or consumed by vain regrets. But what does all this mean? The only thing that is certain, the only thing that will never abandon you is your conscience. It is the only thing that distinguishes man from other living things and makes him closer to God, that makes this life worth living, that lends nobility to man's existence. A conscience allows our deeds to leave their mark, like a furrow in a plowed field, for posterity to judge. O, sweet enchantment, O secret happiness, O paradise, the gift of an immaculate conscience, which I do not possess!"

Amos was thus raving, drunk and emotional. Then his thoughts became confused, lost in a fog ever more dense, and he quickly fell into a deep sleep.

25

❦❦

TIME PASSED SO QUICKLY for Amos and his family.
Everyone was so busy organizing and preparing for June 27, which
was now so close.

On the big day, Amos awoke in his father's house for the last
time. Calm and rested, he got up, slowly got ready, and when he
arrived downstairs, it was almost time for lunch. Everyone was
happy to see him so calm and at ease. Quickly eating a frugal meal,
Amos eventually noticed that a certain tension was growing
around him, and soon everyone was hustling and bustling about, or
at least so it appeared to him. As for Amos, though, he felt as if he
was in a daze; he moved slowly, doing what he was asked, but
unable to shake off the feeling that he was moving in a dream. At
times he felt ridiculous, but suddenly he would find himself capable of completely immersing himself in the role he had to play in
the coming celebration.

Finally, Amos went upstairs to get dressed. He put on a suit
that he had purchased especially for the occasion. Then, as soon as
he was ready, he got into the car with his parents, and they made
their way to the church in Lajatico. As soon as they arrived, he
went to look for Don Carlo, whom he quickly found in the sacristy.
"I want to confess," he said resolutely. The parish priest made

everyone leave, but instead of leading Amos to the confessional, he sat down beside him, inviting him in a friendly way to unburden his heart. It was a brief but intense discussion in which Amos, using all his strength to overcome his own reluctance, embarrassment, and pride, said almost in one breath everything that he knew he had to confess. Then, having received absolution, he reentered the church to check that the musicians had arrived, that his friends who had cameras and video cameras were at their ease and would not disturb the priest, in short, that everything was going well. Finally, he went to find Adriano, who had accepted his invitation to be best man.

Elena wasn't late: at exactly five in the afternoon, she was ready in front of the church. Amos went to meet her, took her by the hand, and together, with faces radiating that special happiness that fills the hearts of those in love and who are about to realize their dream, their common project of life together, and accompanied by the famous opening bars of Mendelssohn's "Wedding March," they crossed the threshold of the church and reached the altar, followed by a festive procession of family and friends.

"I, Elena, take you, Amos, as my husband and promise to be faithful always, in joy and in pain, in sickness and in health..." Amos heard those words and was transported; a joyous smile crept across his lips. A strange thought suddenly came into his head: who knows if his fiancée had really understood the enormity of the promise that he himself would be making to her in a few moments! Why was that solemn promise, so difficult to keep, so utterly necessary? But her voice, sure and serene, a little emotional, which the acoustics of the church rendered mysteriously deep and serious, that voice, so familiar to him, continued: "and to love you and honor you all the days of my life!"

Amos tried to drive those unwonted thoughts from his mind, and instead concentrated on the tone of his own voice, so that it wouldn't sound banal and insincere. So, in a serious but humble tone, without any emphasis, almost hurriedly, he also recited his promise. Ending those phrases, Amos felt a slight light-headed-ness, a sense of bewilderment; then Adriano gave him a tap on the arm, Elena smiled, and he felt suddenly calm.

Leaving the church, Amos and Elena were struck by the number of townspeople, acquaintances, and bystanders who had come to see them, and it was some time before they managed to reach the car. The reception was held in Amos's family home, the house in which he grew up and for which he still felt so much affection. His family and all his closest friends were there, and they all made sure that everything went well: Verano, the baker, always a great friend of Amos's, had made a splendid wedding cake with several layers, topped by an excellent meringue, Amos's favorite sweet, and with other exquisite flavors on the lower layers. Luca and Giorgio had organized an amazing fireworks display, while some of the neighbors helped with serving food and pouring wine.

The party went on into the wee hours of the evening. Saying good-bye to the last guests, the newlyweds finally entered their house, where they had decided to spend their wedding night. Elena was so happy, and on entering their room, she was so moved, she struggled to find the right words to describe her joy, eventually saying only, "It was all exactly what I had always dreamed of!"

The next day they departed for a brief honeymoon: a cruise around the Mediterranean, with stopovers in Spain, Tunisia, Palermo, and Naples, finally disembarking at Genoa, where they had started. The cruise was interesting and exciting for both of them, because neither had traveled on a cruise ship before; in addition, Amos loved the open sea, the mystery of that infinite mass of water, of that infinite space in which the imagination can so completely lose itself. At night, he went out onto the small balcony of their suite, rested his elbows on the railing, and remained there for hours, absorbed in his thoughts, deeply breathing in the exhilarating sea air, which made him feel drunk and woozy.

When they disembarked, before doing anything else, he ran to find a telephone to get news from his parents and Michele, who had promised to do everything possible to arrange for him to go on tour with Zucchero. It was the one thing he still hoped for, and what he now desired the most. However, the now-familiar voice of one of Michele's secretaries informed him that for the moment everything was suspended. Zucchero had decided to release the video of his duet with Pavarotti instead of performing it live. The young woman asked him not to call again; if there was any news, she would take it upon herself to call him.

Amos felt the world fall down around him, and he shut himself away in silence; this saddened Elena, who did not know how to console him. The comfort and optimism of his father and father-in-law, who had come to Genoa to accompany the newlyweds to their beautiful country house, didn't help either. There was nothing to do; even among his friends, Amos continued to be lost in thought and gloomy. Elena left very early every morning to go to work and returned at dinnertime. Amos remained alone, he skipped lunch, practiced piano and singing. Ettore came every day to visit him and together they would read something. Ettore seemed completely unperturbed, and Amos was astounded. Is it possible that he has no comment to make on the situation in which I find myself? he thought to himself, and couldn't find any peace.

Amos passed nearly a whole year in this way, continuing to do the things he always did. But day after day his bewilderment was replaced by resignation, resignation was replaced by peace, and this last restored his energies, his will to do something, his faith in himself and others. Winter arrived. Amos hated the idea of one day soon having to go to his father to ask him to help out. Therefore, as soon as Elena left for work, he immediately turned off the heating and put another sweater on. He made every kind of economic sacrifice he could think of, and this new habit gave him a strength, a capacity for sacrifice, that he had never before known he had.

Elena wanted a baby and spoke to Amos about it ever more frequently. Amos, to tell the truth, had never felt a particular desire to have children, though the idea of a child did intrigue him. But how could he bring a child into this world without first creating the necessary conditions to guarantee it a life rich with opportunity? Therefore he kept putting it off, seeking to dissuade Elena; but every day it became more and more of a fixed idea with her, as the idea of marriage had done earlier.

Amos spent entire days by himself, and it was in this period that he managed finally to impose silence upon himself as an indispensable discipline for an opera singer. All the most celebrated singers of the century had practiced silence and he could not be an exception. When he was alone, silence had a voice that he never tired of listening to, but a voice as well that calmed him and gave him a sense of well-being. But his first attempts to be silent among other people were very difficult; not being able to have his say, having to submit to the opinions of others without answering, expressing himself, was for him a true punishment. But those first harsh criticisms he had suffered, the first disappointments, the always more concrete fears of seeing his dreams finally going up in smoke, rendered him stronger and more determined.

No one understood the necessity of this eccentricity; so instead of encouragement, he found everyone laughing at him, and exhorting him to forget about it. For this reason, Amos spent most of his time alone, within the walls of his house, where the silence caressed his spirit and spoke to him in a reassuring voice: "Try to give your best, to be honest in judging yourself and others, listen to your conscience and go forward in strength, because goodwill and the spirit of sacrifice in the end always pay off!"

Amos walked back and forth in his room smiling at the almost infantile simplicity of those concepts and thinking, These are things that our teachers used to say, that my grandmother used to lecture me about when I was a child, that my catechism teacher used to repeat . . . ! But still the voice spoke to him: "There is more simple truth in these things than in the obscure speeches of politicians, in those confused and abstract pronouncements of bureaucrats, in the presumptuous and fatuous words of men of science, or worse, in the cynical and sinister sentences of the men of the law . . ."

In a letter to his singing teacher, Amos wrote: "I can't thank you enough for recommending the discipline of silence; it certainly helps the voice, but it helps the spirit even more; when I am alone silence teaches the spirit to know itself better, and to understand others much better than when one responds with an answering torrent of words. How many absurdities and foolishnesses are said in the course of a conversation, and on the other hand, how many important things are lost because we simply haven't listened hard enough, and fear only not saying enough ourselves, or not being sufficiently persuasive! I have learned so many things, maestro, and I'm sure there are many more surprises reserved for me in the future by the music of silence!"

Amos received an enormous satisfaction from studying music and developing of his voice, which in some way balanced out all of his worries about not yet having realized his dreams. When someone invited him to leave his isolation, to let go and enjoy himself a bit, Amos, smiling, would respond that he was very happy with his simple existence, that he had need of nothing. He thought to himself, The worth of an artist is in inverse proportion to the extent of his needs, his follies, and his desires, because the true artist is nourished entirely by his art and that is enough to make him happy and completely satisfied.

Besides, who would it please if he became rich? Amos believed that in his frenetic race to enrich himself, a man begins, it is true, by possessing the indispensable, then the useful, then the superfluous; but he is still not happy, so money becomes first potentially dangerous then actually damaging, if not for him, who often doesn't even find the time to spend it, surely for the members of his family.

At long last, that winter, which for Amos was one of the longest and coldest he could remember, passed into spring. In the meantime, as he had promised himself, he had completed his study of the celebrated Sonata in D Minor by Bach, transcribed by Busoni for the piano. It was a surprising result, because his playing was still far from perfect. With the beginning of spring he had decided to permit himself a romantic interlude, studying the Nocturne no. 3 by Franz Liszt, better known as the "Dream of Love." He threw himself into it, with joy and passion. He quickly memorized it, before concentrating on perfecting the more complicated passages.

❦

One day he was completely immersed in studying a cadenza when he heard the telephone ring. It was the last thing he needed. Unwillingly, he got up and ran to the phone, not liking the idea of not knowing who was calling and not believing his ears when he recognized Michele's voice. "I have some good news for you," he said. "This time, I think I did it; prepare yourself to leave toward the end of May for a tour of Italy, in the most important soccer stadiums."

Amos was speechless. He couldn't believe his own ears! But he quickly called his wife and then his parents, unsuccessfully covering up an uncontrollable enthusiasm. Yet a sudden thought struck him; at the end of May there was a very important singing course, directed by a famous Italian soprano, who had warmly invited him to participate. So what was he to do? Which was he to turn down? Why did fate conspire so much against him? These were the first important steps in his career, and he was now forced to choose between them.

Desperately Amos thought of Ettore, wanting to get some advice from him, but then, thinking about it, he immediately imagined Ettore's response; "In cases like this," he would say, "the best advice that one can give is to not accept advice from anyone." So he went to see his father and put the question to him. Mr. Bardi breathed deeply, and also seemed undecided. Then he said: "Amos, you have to decide by yourself so that no one takes the responsibility of advising you. At times like these everyone is alone with themselves." Having said that, he passed a hand through his son's hair, a gesture that filled Amos's heart with tenderness.

Amos knew that his father would have shed his own blood to see his son happy. Poor Father! he thought. He immediately wanted to console him. Well! Listen, better two opportunities than none! Then, reasoning to himself, Amos thought, and if I lose this battle will I force my father to continue working until I do? No! This isn't right! If things go badly again, I will look for any job at all, I will be a telephone operator, a masseur, bank clerk, but this situation *must* end now. This is my last chance at a singing career.

Women, it must be admitted, are often more practical and efficient than men. Mrs. Bardi and Elena did not hesitate to advise Amos to opt for Michele's proposal, which would produce immediate and concrete results. The other idea was expensive and held only promises. Shamefacedly, Amos decided to call the famous singer to tell her of his decision, without giving any reasons or explanations. The woman, sounding annoyed, listed the opportunities that Amos would miss out on in a reproving tone of voice; finally, though, she seemed resigned, and with a slightly frosty tone she said good-bye.

The days passed, and to Amos—who had a terrifying sense of misgiving—they seemed eternal. A concert at the town's theater was all that lay between him and the tour, and again he feared the worst: at the rehearsal, Amos inadvertently fell from the stage, ending up in the first row of seats, but fortunately he was only slightly hurt.

The next day, accompanied by Elena, as happy as she was incredulous, he left for Bassano del Grappa, where, for the first time, he would sing a duet with Zucchero in what was to be the high point of the concert. Amos was therefore to be brought to the

public's attention thanks to the efforts of one of the most celebrated tenors in the world. How would almost fifteen thousand
listeners react to the duet? This is what Amos asked himself,
before appearing onstage, seated at the piano, on a mechanized
platform. But the public almost always likes novelty; so Amos's
first tremulous notes were received with an authentic ovation. At
the end of the piece, the crowd seemed literally crazed. Fifteen
thousand deafening voices were crying out, drowning even the
sound from the enormous amplifiers, and the next day, in the arts
section of a famous daily newspaper, there appeared a headline
that was to remain forever impressed in the memory of the entire
Bardi family: AMOS BARDI DOESN'T DISAPPOINT MAESTRO
PAVAROTTI.

Full of emotion and moved almost to tears, Amos had finally
won his first, real battle.

26

❧❧

EVIDENTLY SOMETHING WAS HAPPENING in the stars, fate was conspiring in Amos's favor. In the meantime, unaware and incredulous, he proceeded as always along his own path, a path forged in years of doubt and disappointment, to which he was now so used that he preferred it to any deceitful hope and certainty. But now his road was becoming slowly paved with some frail hopes, grounded in his knowledge of his own capacities and his own spirit of sacrifice.

Zucchero's concert tour was a real triumph. Amos left the stage every night accompanied by a deafening ovation that filled him with joy and almost made him drunk; then, in the dressing room, he would find Elena waiting for him, also happy and incredulous. In little less than a month they traveled the length of Italy from north to south in a bus overflowing with musicians and suitcases, without even the comfort of air-conditioning. And yet Amos was so excited that he even found himself amazed at the ill humor of some of his colleagues, who were wilting from the heat. He, meanwhile, felt as though he were in a dream; indeed, sometimes he felt as though he would awaken at any moment to find himself in his bed at home, with all his old problems. Instead he found himself really on tour, and was even paid a salary that would have been sufficient for an entire year's worth of expenses. He felt enraptured, full of an inexhaustible energy that amazed even himself. He was always ready to go, to strengthen the ties of friendship with his traveling companions; he was never sleepy and at night would daydream about the strange rapport between his own past and his future. He tried to see into the future, and didn't know how to forgive himself for the negative judgments and lack of faith in himself he had felt until that moment. But he had had patience, he had never lost courage and had never completely lost his optimism. Perhaps for these reasons, fortune was just now beginning to repay him.

That summer was really hot; sometimes he would get out of bed and open the refrigerator for a beer; then, overcoming every temptation, he would close it and satisfy himself with a glass of water from the bathroom tap, and continue his own nightly meditations. How unjust I am! he thought. I wasn't content with life, even though it saved me from every danger and kept me from the easy victories which not only don't pay but are so damaging as well. What a fool I've been.

Everyone quickly became his friend. Zucchero himself, more than once, invited him to dinner, and when he was due to appear on an eagerly awaited television program, he agreed to Amos's timid suggestion that he replace the keyboard player, who had fallen ill the day before. Zucchero thought for a moment, but then agreed; indeed he even decided to sing the same song that he sang with Amos in a duet during the concert tour. So in this way even the doors of television were opened to Amos; it was what his father had always hoped for, and it helped Michele to judge whether Amos was telegenic or, to use an expression of the trade, if he "broke the videotape." The result—as everyone admitted— was a success beyond every expectation, and the next day, in the newspaper, the television ratings showed that during the piece Amos had sung with Zucchero, there was a striking and unforeseen increase in viewers.

A few days before the end of the tour, Amos received a piece of news that left him mad with joy and trepidation: in Turin there would be a singing course, led by the famous tenor Franco Corelli. Could it be true? Was it possible that Corelli would stand before the students in person and speak to them about singing? Amos couldn't believe it; and yet his parents, by phone, assured him it was true. There would be a selection process, conducted by a jury of experts, then the maestro would arrive. Amos begged his parents to enroll him in the course and prepared himself to confront any obstacles that might block his meeting with the man who, more than anyone else, had spoken to his heart and had moved him to tears through his extraordinary voice.

The last day of the tour was perhaps the most emotional for Amos because the performance took place in the communal stadium of Florence; that is, in his own province of Tuscany. All his friends were there, as well as many relatives. In his dressing room his heart was beating fast. When he reached the stage, in the midst of all that uproar, he heard his name called out. Someone wanted to express his affection and be—in some way—closer to him. At the end of the concert he was finally able to embrace his family, whom he had not seen since the first day of the tour, and that night he returned home, but only for a day. He had time only to repack his suitcases and return to Turin for Corelli's singing course, for the first time since his wedding without the company of his wife, to limit the cost of the trip.

He arrived in Turin late at night, accompanied by his father, who would depart the next morning, and he quickly went to the small convent where a friend had found lodgings for him. The room was small and bare, very different from the rooms in the great hotels in which he had sometimes stayed during the tour, but Amos didn't care; he thought only about the moment when he would meet his maestro, and that was sufficient. In the morning, when his father had left, Amos went with other hopefuls to the Press Circle where the first tryouts would be held. He had decided to remain even if he was rejected: he would then at least hear the words of Maestro Corelli and his precious advice.

When it was his turn, he entered the great hall full of tension, which was easily read on his face; he leaned on the piano and, without further ado, performed the famous aria from *Arlesiana* of Francesco Cilea, "Il Lamento di Federico." At the end of the piece, he left the hall with his head bowed, accompanied by the pianist, and prepared himself to await the result of his first audition. Out of approximately one hundred who had signed up, only twelve young singers would have the opportunity to take the course; a harsh selection that would conclude that very night. Amos felt an unrestrainable joy when, from the voice of the president of the jury, he heard his name among those accepted.

Maestro Corelli arrived a few days later by train. Amos and a companion in the class, full of impatience, went to meet him at the train station. The maestro and his wife were among the last to descend from the train and it seemed to Amos that when he finally was before him, able to shake his hand, it must all be a dream. Having settled the maestro's suitcases in the trunk of a taxi, Amos and his friend respectfully said good-bye and ran to the Press Circle, where soon the first lesson would take place by one of the most celebrated singers of the century.

When Maestro Corelli made his entrance into the great hall, overflowing with fans, journalists, photographers, and young singers, thunderous applause accompanied him until he reached his place on a small stage near the piano. The maestro sat down at the piano and greeted everyone. He didn't make any introductory remarks or speech; one could see that he was embarrassed, and that he would have preferred to have been anywhere but there under the gaze of all those people, who hung on his every word and were impatient to hear him speak.

"Who would like to sing first?" asked the maestro. There was a long silence. Everyone looked at Amos, by now knowing of his love, admiration, and strange capacity for imitating Corelli; but

Amos didn't move; indeed he tried to make himself as small as possible. So then a girl in the first row got up and bravely went toward the piano, greeted the maestro, and announced that she would sing a Puccini aria from *La Rondine;* she put the music at the piano and began. The execution was uncertain, the voice was small, unsteady, and labored, especially on the high notes. When she was finished Corelli appeared to everyone embarrassed and hesitant. "You have a singing teacher?" he asked her. She nodded yes. "And you *pay* such a teacher?" added Corelli, his gaze fixed on the floor, as if he were speaking to himself. Tears came to the eyes of the poor girl, who ran back to her seat, covering her face.

The maestro was visibly sorry for what he had just said, but there was nothing more to say or do. So, to cover his own state of mind, he breathed deeply and asked: "I would like to hear a tenor." Amos's friend—the one who had accompanied him to the train station and who was now seated by his side—took him by the arm and pushed him forward. Amos tried to resist but Maestro Corelli saw the entire scene, recognized Amos, and invited him to get up. Amos obeyed: with his heart in his throat he took two steps and found himself by the piano. Confusedly he said he would sing Rodolfo's famous aria from Puccini's *La Bohème,* and he quickly heard the first notes of the aria. As if in a dream, he now found himself singing in front of his idol, his favorite singer, and he felt utterly bewildered. He sang without even the least awareness of what he was doing, and when he was finished he was struck by the silence in the hall that awoke him the same way a violent cry reawakens a man in the midst of sleep.

Seconds passed which felt like hours. The maestro moved toward him, placed a hand on his shoulder, and said: "The voice is very beautiful; I believe I can give you some useful suggestions."

Amos listened in disbelief; by now he had come to his senses and was capable of a certain semblance of calmness. He thanked Corelli with a trembling voice and then asked to be excused for a moment; his shirt was soaked with sweat and he wanted to drink some cold water, but he was happy to have passed the test, and now he felt more sure of himself. He ran to the men's room and took off his shirt, wrung it out, and put it back on; it was completely rumpled, but what could he do? He drank a few sips of water and silently reentered the hall, where he cautiously reached his seat. Corelli was saying something, but when he saw Amos he stopped, called Amos over to him, and invited him to perform the Puccini aria again. This time, though, he interrupted him after every phrase and spoke about singing techniques, he gave very short examples and asked Amos to repeat this or that phrase with the technical devices and interpretations that he had suggested, until the end of the lesson. Amos was exhausted but happy.

At the exit Mrs. Corelli stopped Amos and complimented him, and he felt encouraged enough to ask permission to come and pay the Corellis a visit at home, after the course, to have private lessons. In this way, Amos would have the opportunity to establish a rapport that for him was extremely important. The signora, without hesitating, reassured him on the good impression he had made on her husband, who would surely be happy to meet him again.

The course concluded with a concert by the five best pupils. Amos performed the same aria, which he had studied intensely in those days with the maestro. The next day in the Turin newspaper, an interview was published with Maestro Corelli on his impressions about the level of the students in the course and his thoughts about lyrical singing. The maestro said he was satisfied with the interest expressed by the student singers, and even said that he had been particularly struck by a tenor by the name of Amos Bardi whose singing had given him a real thrill because he possessed a voice full of pathos, a sweet and sad voice that really moved the public. Amos couldn't believe his ears when a friend from the course, just before his departure, read him the article. Like a child, he grabbed the newspaper from the hands of his friend and clutched it to his chest, swearing that he would keep it forever.

In what felt like only a moment his life had been completely transformed. From that monotonous and solitary existence to which he had been resigned, Amos had suddenly passed to a life of continuous excitement. He was still young, strong-willed, full of energy and enthusiasm, and the turmoil of events not only didn't worry him, but even reenergized and inspired him, or, to be more precise, it brought out all of the things that until then had remained hidden in his being and his manner of presenting himself to others.

❧❧

Soon after arriving home, Amos found a message from Michele, urging him to come to Milan the next day to have a meeting with a record company which, following Amos's successful tour with Zucchero, had demonstrated a genuine interest in him. There was a real possibility of finally reaching an agreement that would lead to working on an interesting project. Naturally Amos didn't need to be told twice, and left with his father and Elena for Milan, where he had the opportunity of meeting the president of the company, whom he had often in the past tried to reach, but without success.

He was made at home in an office that seemed to him extremely spacious and bright. The president, who was a very distinguished and professional middle-aged woman named Caterina, invited him to sit down and sang his praises, describing her feelings when she had first heard his warm and expressive voice, which had given her goose bumps and immediately convinced her that it was necessary to take that voice to the masses. She was ready to begin work; indeed, she had spoken with some of the musicians and writers she worked with and already had a song ready, an extraordinary piece, which, she thought, Amos could present at the Festival of San Remo. Amos buried his head in his hands to hide his emotion: how many attempts, how many disappointed hopes, how many humiliations had he suffered; and now, all of a sudden, someone had turned the page.

Amos had always been something of an optimist, but he was just not used to believing in so much good fortune, and part of him didn't *want* to believe. But he liked the song, and in addition, it seemed very suited to his voice. Amos recorded it with results that amazed everyone. Even Michele was pleased; finally, a record executive had had faith in him, and Amos couldn't wait for the moment when he could show everyone who had ever closed a door in his face that he had been right all along. Then, too, the enthusiasm of the record company was infectious, even to an old hand like Michele.

In the blink of an eye, all the decisions had been made; all difficulties smoothed over, including those of a contractual nature: the company, as always happened in these cases, imposed its rules. For his part, Amos made a tremendous effort, and contrary to all his principles and all that he had learned in the course of long years of study and sacrifice, decided to treat the adventure that had just begun as no more than a great game, which shouldn't be taken too seriously.

It was November 1990, and at San Remo Amos was among the so-called new acts taking part in the first rounds. In the midst of all that confusion and all those excited and ambitious people, he wasn't, to tell the truth, at ease, and he stayed on his own, more or less shut in his hotel room with Elena, who never left him for a moment and sought to reassure him with her constant love and care. But Amos was tense and inexplicably introverted; above all, he feared the vote of the popular juries, almost completely made up of young people. What would those kids, so used to listening to louder and more modern music, think of his calm and clean voice and his style of singing, which was, in some ways, old-fashioned? But in the silence of the night these thoughts were overcome by the sensation, difficult to explain, of being safe, protected by a favorable star, driven by a good wind toward the promised goal.

The contestants were first invited to present a well-known piece. Amos had no indecision about the choice: he would sing the song that had brought him so much luck until that moment performing both the part of Zucchero as well as the tenor part, which was well known to the public through the voice of the maestro Pavarotti. Surely that, at least, would be a surprise, and the extreme flexibility of his voice had to impress the jury. Already during his afternoon rehearsals he had noted the reaction of those present, and he felt more relaxed.

That evening, Amos was one of the last to go onstage. The public was already more or less sated with music, with voices and with new faces, and barely noticed his entrance onto the stage; indeed, they listened distractedly to his introduction and someone even let out an exclamation of derision when the master of ceremonies announced that Amos would perform, alone, both Zucchero's and Pavarotti's part. Then the orchestra began and Amos's voice resounded in the hall, strong and full; the entire auditorium fell silent to listen to him. After a few bars, Amos changed registers: his voice shifted completely in timbre and intonation, and a hurricane of spontaneous and unstoppable applause rose from the hall. Meanwhile, in a reserved room in a hotel not far from the theater, Michele and his colleagues and some friends were following the show on television with bated breath. Some had tears in their eyes; others held them back with difficulty, and Stefano, one of Amos's strongest supporters, was feeling ill. At the end of the piece, the entire audience rose to its feet and submerged the last notes of the orchestra with applause and delirious cries.

It was done. Even Amos was convinced, and suddenly he wasn't worried anymore about the jury's verdict.

In the three months before the festival in San Remo, Amos had returned to his regular life, except with a bit more energy: now he felt that he was fighting for a concrete opportunity, not merely a remote hope of success. A new strength had overtaken him and a new faith in himself conferred a strange sensation that, from that moment, everything that he would undertake would turn out well. But how could he explain this sudden change in the circumstances of his own life? There were no explicit, comprehensible reasons, or at least Amos couldn't discern them. In a few days, he began to record his first album in a studio in Bologna. It wasn't easy to find the perfect songs for his voice, but eventually the right material was brought together. Amos threw himself into it with all his strength, and soon he had a pretty good understanding of what would prove to be the decisive album of his career.

One day, while practicing a piece on the piano, a businessman, a friend of the owner of the studio, happened to be there; he heard Amos's voice, stopped to listen, and remained as if hypnotized by that sound, which he was hearing for the very first time. He made some inquiries about the name of the singer and was told it was a young tenor by the name of Amos Bardi, a participant at the San Remo Festival as a new act, and who was recording an album. Mr. Monti was a skillful entrepreneur, intelligent and instinctive, but also a generous and sensitive patron of the arts; with the swiftness of lightning and without even bothering to meet the artist who had made such an impression on him, he asked his friend to convince Amos to sing in a concert at the theater in Reggio Emilia, his city, with the support of a good orchestra and an excellent conductor. He would absorb all the costs, including the organization of the event, down to the last detail.

To sing in a traditional theater accompanied by an orchestra was something that Amos had always dreamed of. Mr. Monti worked hard at his extravagant enterprise at the theater, but he was told that not even a famous tenor could pull in more than three hundred spectators, much less some unknown crooner from the provinces who was preparing to participate in the festival. But Mr. Monti wasn't the type to back down, and did everything that was necessary, including making sure there was a full house by inviting—at his expense—friends, music lovers, colleagues, and employees from his businesses to come and listen to what he, without any fear of contradiction, by now called the most beautiful voice he had ever heard. Thanks to his extraordinary power of persuasion, everyone agreed without hesitation. On the day of the concert, the theater was overcrowded, to the joy of Mr. Monti and the chagrin of those who had doubted him.

Everything was ready. Amos, shut in his small dressing room and feeling nervous, warmed up his voice and had the impression that he was not in the best of vocal conditions. He had ice-cold hands and was in a cold sweat under the apprehensive gaze of Elena and the desperate gaze of his mother. All of a sudden there was a knock on the door and they heard a voice that echoed down the entire hallway: "You're on!" Amos went to the stage with legs that almost wouldn't carry him. He began to sing, and gave it everything he had. The public greeted him with affection and empathy, but his voice was still not supported by a steel diaphragm and a solid technique; thus, at the end of the concert, despite the applause and the handshakes, Amos felt that things definitely had not gone as well as he and his generous friend, Mr. Monti, had hoped.

27

FEBRUARY ARRIVED. One fine morning a car reached Poggioncino, sent by the record company to take Amos and Elena to Rome, where he was to participate in an important television program to be screened before the finals of the San Remo Festival. That morning the entire family was together. Mr. Bardi waited for Amos, who came down the stairs with his own suitcase and a duffel bag on his shoulders, helped him place the suitcases into the trunk of the car, then embraced him with such emotion that Amos was surprised. His mother, usually more emotional than her husband, preferred this time to play the part of the courageous woman who doesn't let herself be swept away by events, even when they are extraordinary; so she said good-bye to the couple with studied calm. Amos knew her attitude well and felt a rush of tenderness. Poor Mamma! he thought. Who knows what she is feeling at this moment and how hard she tries to give me strength! Then, to overcome his emotions, Amos said good-bye and quickly climbed into the car, closed the door, and tried to distract himself by adjusting the position of the seat.

In Rome, there wasn't even time to deposit the suitcases at the hotel or to freshen up; therefore, the driver went directly to Parioli, accompanied the Bardi couple to the theater, and left.

A young woman led them to the dressing room, brought some mineral water, offered them coffee, and then explained that in a few minutes someone would call Amos to make up. "Why the long face?" asked the makeup woman; Amos evidently didn't appreciate all that attention to his skin and face, the smell of the cosmetics, the sticky dust. And to imagine that the woman was there only to give him some color! "Nothing, nothing, miss! Don't worry!" Amos answered, smiling. "It's just that I'm not used to this and to tell the truth, I'm a bit embarrassed . . ."

Finally the curtain was raised and the host began to introduce his guests. When it was Amos's turn he got up and, urged on by the host, sang a song from his first record. It was the Italian version of an old South American classic: a simple and easy-to-listen-to melody, to which he added all the passion of his character and all his youthful energy. The audience exploded into thunderous applause even before the song was finished. Seated in the audience, right at the back, Michele could not believe his eyes, and confessed to himself that he just couldn't explain the public's incredible reaction to Amos's voice.

At the end of the taping another car was waiting to take Amos and Elena to the central railway station in Rome. A big fat driver, puffing and wheezing, urged them to hurry so as not to miss the train. He was the cheerful and loquacious type; he wanted to know everything about Amos's plans, and promised to follow the San Remo Festival on television and cheer for Amos. Amos smiled, but he had other concerns. Reaching the station, they collected their tickets and ran to the platform, where the train was by now ready for departure. Carrying their suitcases and with tickets in hand, they tried to find the sleeping car where they would spend the night. Amos would have liked to ask someone for help, but the station was already far behind them. The train was so long that the idea of having to walk its entire length was discouraging; at that moment of nervous exhaustion Amos had the sensation of being abandoned and of running against the motion of the train as one struggles against destiny: alone and defenseless.

Amos and Elena finally found their places. It was so hot that the air in the compartment was practically unbreathable. They put away their bags, then Amos quickly stretched out in one of the sleeping compartments. Even though it was far too small for his body, given his exhaustion, it was comfortable enough. Elena lay down in the berth below, and both of them were silent, not because they had nothing to say to each other; on the contrary, perhaps they had too many things to say, so many emotions that silence became the most direct and efficient language to express what words would have rendered banal and inadequate.

Amos tried to sleep but was too agitated. A flood of memories filled his mind; he heard voices from near and far away in time, phrases that encouraged him, and those that upset him, that intimidated him; he had the strange sensation of traveling to a place where he would finally prove something to everyone, but he didn't yet know if he would emerge victorious or defeated. Personal pride struggled with common sense and he heard once again the voice of Ettore, who warned him: "Never take anything too seriously!"

In the meantime, the train proceeded slowly, rumbling monotonously. The conductor had already passed to check their tickets, advising the passengers to shut themselves up in their compartments before falling asleep to avoid any ugly surprises on awakening. The train stopped very often, and Amos was still awake when he heard the loudspeaker announce that they were arriving at Pisa. I could just get off here, in my own city, and decide myself in what direction to take my life! But why do I feel as though I don't have the strength to do it? Why do I prefer this idea of remaining curled up in this sleeping berth, letting myself be taken wherever it decides? he thought. The train departed almost immediately. Amos turned over onto his other side. A sudden tiredness finally defeated him; he closed his eyes and fell asleep.

28

WHEN THE TRAIN STOPPED at the San Remo station, Amos and Elena were among the first to leave the carriage. Outside a beautiful sun was shining and a light breeze from the sea blew the last traces of sleep from their faces. Amos's gloomy sense of solitude and bewilderment had now been left behind. The train was already leaving when what seemed to be a very young and friendly woman came forward to meet them, greeting them cheerfully. She was Delfina, an employee of the record company who had the task of assisting Amos for the duration of the festival, and organizing his working day, which was full of commitments.

"You have just enough time to put your suitcases away and freshen up a bit, then the radio interviews begin, three I think, so that makes four meetings with the press altogether," said Delfina, smiling with satisfaction at her work. Amos was radiant with joy. All these things to do were a blessing; too bad there weren't more! He felt great, full of strength, as if nothing could stop him. The test that everyone was waiting for was about to take place; his life's dream, what everyone had encouraged him to dream about ever since he was a child, was about to happen. He was aware of it, yet he was tranquil; he breathed in deeply the briny air and prepared to fulfill his duty as best he could. Unbeknownst to him, everyone was by now speaking about him as the probable winner of the festival, but no one in the business seriously believed in the success of the record. "He'll cause some excitement in the hall," it was said, "but he won't sell a single record." Only Caterina really believed; as president, she had done everything to convince her colleagues, defending the project tooth and nail, with her passionate temperament and tenacity as an ex-artist. She, along with Michele, had done everything possible; now she crossed her fingers and waited to see how things would turn out.

Amos, in the meantime, slowly but surely made himself known, not only as a singer but also as a person who always gave his all, without the need to put on a front or succumb to the blandishments of the press. He was a son of the countryside, the product of a simple education, which thanks to Ettore had become even more deeply rooted in him. He always answered journalists with total candor, because that was the simplest and surest way. During a press conference one of them stood up and harshly attacked the so-called new acts category, from which, he said, nothing new and nothing really original had come, and he invited each participant to justify in some way their presence in a show that was without doubt the most important in radio and television. It was pure provocation, an unpleasant question to which everyone answered with some difficulty and embarrassment. When it was Amos's turn, he calmly said, "To tell the truth, I have always been occupied in courting the truly beautiful, rather than prostituting myself to the illusions and flattery of the simply new." He had not even completed his answer when thunderous applause rose up to greet his skillful rebuttal. The next day almost all the Italian daily newspapers, which always dedicated an enormous amount of space to the festival because it was the most popular singing event of the year, reported Amos's words; one of them carried this headline on the show-business page: BARDI SPEAKS OUT: A FEW WORDS AND ALREADY HE'S A FIGURE TO BE

RECKONED WITH. And to a famous journalist who had harshly criticized the poverty of content of the songs during the festival, citing Amos among others, Amos responded: "Who knows, perhaps he's right; in any event, there are those who *do* and those who simply *criticize* and I prefer to take my chances among those who *do*."

In the meantime, the tension increased; one breathed it everywhere. Amos, filled with curiosity, tried to understand what was going on and at the same time to somehow remain above the fray. The contestants were excessively nervous, or excessively generous, excessively loquacious, or excessively silent; no matter what, they were always excessive. Everyone tried to adopt a reserved attitude, to appear calm and in control of themselves, but every gesture, every word, betrayed an ill-concealed state of agitation. All everyone spoke about was the festival, the gossip and rumors, the behind-the-scene scenes, as if there were nothing more important in the entire world. Amos understood perfectly well what was happening, and in some ways he laughed, but slowly, inevitably, even he felt himself becoming involved, caught in a trap, contaminated by that incandescent atmosphere. He would often retreat to his hotel room and try to think of other things, of what Ettore would have advised him to do.

Who knows what Ettore made of the adventures of his young friend! In Lajatico, he was continuing his usual life, serene and imperturbable. Since his departure, Amos had not heard a word from him; a good sign, it meant that Ettore approved of what Amos was doing and had nothing to suggest. Amos often tried to imagine what Ettore was thinking, and that particular mental voyage calmed him and made him feel sure of himself.

Time passed and the final day of the festival approached, that last Saturday in February when twenty million television viewers would hear his voice, see him, and judge him. And it was those twenty million people who would decide his destiny in just a few minutes; he knew this very well but tried to think of something else.

On Friday, his parents, aunts, and uncles arrived in San Remo. His dearest friends had decided to remain at home to follow the festival on television. Amos often thought of them and felt that they were with him, that they suffered and hoped by his side: Adriano and Verano would surely be together in front of the television with their hearts beating hard, but even in his town, in Lajatico, everyone would be cheering for him. At nearby Sterza, in fact, in an industrial hangar, a huge screen had been set up, and hundreds of chairs brought in. Amos's heart beat hard at the thought of all the people who were close to him, how they trembled and suffered with him. As for the others, he didn't give them a single thought; the ones who had made fun of his aspirations, his attempts that had gone up in smoke, or especially the ones who had tried to discourage him; for them he didn't even give a moment of his time, convinced as he was of the necessity of thinking positively, especially during those most important moments.

❧❦

Finally Saturday arrived. Amos passed the day completely alone, shut up in his room in the most rigorous silence. When Delfina came to call on him, she was amazed to find him so remote from the atmosphere that prevailed outside his hotel room. Amos had not even switched on the television to follow the festival, which had already started an hour before.

It was already late, and they had to rush to the theater. A taxi waited for them at the entrance of the hotel. Amos got in the back and Delfina sat in the front and gave instructions to the driver. The traffic was infernal. The people were packed on the pavements; everyone wanted to get a glimpse of the artists from up close, and would break into cries and shouts when they thought they saw someone famous in the luxurious cars that went back and forth before their eyes.

Getting out of the taxi, Amos made his way through the crowd, which hardly recognized him, and ran to his dressing room. He had barely enough time to warm up his voice, and almost immediately it was his turn. Elena was at his side and she gripped his arm. On his other side was Caterina, who was also visibly emotional: after all the battles undertaken on behalf of their dream, one that was outside the range of what was generally fashionable at the time, she was also preparing herself for Amos's big moment, and she wasn't able to maintain her calm as much as she would have liked.

Elena was silent, and swallowed in an attempt to clear the lump in her throat that felt like it was suffocating her. When she heard Amos's name and realized that she had to let him go, she was overwhelmed with emotion. I have always been at your side, I have loved you and am ready to face anything with you! she thought. But what can I do for you now but remain here and wait? Now everything is in your hands; go and let happen what may; *go*, my love!

Mrs. Bardi was seated, or more precisely curled up, in a seat in the front row, her feelings not very different from those of her daughter-in-law. In cases like this, conjugal love and maternal love have many elements in common: they are both painful and absolutely sincere. Mrs. Bardi, too, felt an anguished sense of impotence when she embraced her son with her eyes as he was sitting down at the piano and placed his fingers on the keys. She would have liked to adjust his hair, fix the collar of his shirt, perhaps unbutton a button on his jacket, suggest that he hold his head higher, to remain calm; a prayer, very short but intense, occupied her attention for a moment. She clenched her fists, bit her lip, then sat immobile, as if drained of strength and will. Only her gaze remained luminous, stubbornly fixed on her son, and her wide eyes appeared to project rays of hope, joy, energy, fear, passion, and agitation.

Amos, meanwhile, had begun to sing with his usual passion, with that unique ability to identify himself with the music that made him stand out. He began the introduction almost timidly but then found all the force and warmth that his voice could produce, and the effect was immediate: from the hall a thunderous applause rose. Elena and Caterina, standing behind the curtains at the side of the stage, were following the performance on a television monitor. They didn't dare take their eyes off it, lest they lose their grip on their emotions.

Amos, by now calm and sure of himself, put an energy and a force into every word that amazed even himself, allowing him to change tonality in such a way that an unstoppable enthusiasm began to take hold of the audience: someone yelled out a cry of acclamation, some got to their feet, and on the final note—which the conductor held for an unusually long time—everyone was on their feet. The applause and the cries were deafening; many members of the audience had tears in their eyes and the emcee wasn't able to restore order for some time.

Backstage, Amos quickly found Elena, and without saying anything they walked back toward the dressing room. But on the stairs she stopped suddenly, and grabbing with both hands the lapels of Amos's open jacket, she buried her face in his chest and burst into sobs. Caterina, who was following behind, saw the scene. Continuing toward them, she reached the stairs, gently patted Amos's back as she passed, but didn't stop, perhaps so as not to disturb that moment of intimate emotion, which had something so romantic and rare about it.

❧

A little later Amos was taken, together with all the other contestants, to another floor, where they would wait for the results of the final voting. They were led down a narrow hallway, with numerous small doors on each side that opened into bare little rooms, one for each contestant. In his room, Amos found only a chair. He sat down and took Elena on his knee. Through the plywood walls that divided those cubbyholes, the music of an acoustic guitar reached Amos; it was the person in the next room who was playing to pass the time and exorcise the tension, which grew moment by moment. There was nothing to do and nothing to say. Every word sounded useless and ridiculous. Every once in a while there was a cry of acclamation, but they were just false alarms.

All of a sudden someone knocked at the door of Amos's room; it was Barbara, a friend of Delfina's, who also worked for the record company. "Come," she said, smiling, "we have to go up quickly."

"Why?" asked Amos, a bit impatiently.

"What do you mean? Don't you know?" she asked, incredulous.

"No!" answered Amos. "They told me to wait here for five or ten minutes, but we've been here—"

Barbara interrupted him: "*You've won, Amos!* You've won and no one has told you yet! You have to go onstage, they sent me to get you!"

For a moment Amos felt as though he were dreaming. He was slightly bewildered and didn't know what to say. Finally he pulled himself together. "Then let's go!" he said calmly. Around him were all the other contestants, and he didn't want to upset them with foolish displays of exuberance. He took Barbara's hand and walked toward the stairs, followed by Elena. Everyone shook his hand and congratulated him. On the top floor he was stopped by reporters from the three most important news agencies. "A first impression, Bardi: what do you feel right now and who are you thinking of?"

"What do I feel?" answered Amos. "I really don't know how to explain, but my thoughts go out to all my friends, to all those who share with me this enormous joy; to those who are far away physically but close to me emotionally."

Millions of viewers meanwhile were glued to their television sets and were anxiously awaiting the name of the winner. In the midst of the confusion, Amos seemed to hear the voice of the emcee, who was saying: "In tenth place . . ." He strained his ears but wasn't able to hear the name of the contestant. With some difficulty they made their way through the press of people toward the backstage area. They pulled back a heavy curtain and went forward a few more steps. Everyone was by now behind the curtains, and from there the voice of the host reached them clearly. "In seventh place . . ." The emcee paused to increase the tension and electrify the audience.

Amos thought of his parents, who wouldn't know anything yet and were suffering terribly, struggling between hope and fear, but he could do absolutely nothing for them. He imagined them sunk in their seats with their brows covered in sweat and their hands ice cold, their throats dry, and tears in their eyes. In reality, Mr. Bardi had gotten up and had gone toward the back of the theater to wait with his hands behind his back, leaning against the wall, avoiding the looks of the people who at that moment were all focused on the stage.

After announcing the third-place winner, the emcee—an old hand—interrupted himself; there was a long pause while he called an assistant, whom he asked to guess the name of the winner. Meanwhile a group of technicians ran to move the piano to where it had been during Amos's performance. Mr. Bardi noted all this and felt relieved: after the announcement, the winner would probably sing the same song he or she had sung in the contest; therefore, if the piano was being moved, the winner was surely his son. He felt at a loss only for a moment, before Amos's name resounded throughout the hall, accompanied by a massive ovation from the audience. Mr. Bardi tried to applaud with the others but then turned his face to the wall as if he were seeking an exit, to be alone with himself and to fully savor that moment, which seemed truly incredible, but was absolutely real. So many battles, so many disillusionments, so many worries for his son's future; a son who seemed to him born to sing and yet who couldn't seem to find the path to translate that great passion into the something from which he could earn a living! And just when he had found himself on the point of losing all hope, everything had happened as if in a dream!

At that precise moment the audience was on its feet, declaring Amos the winner of the most important Italian music festival. It was enough to drive one mad with joy. But seeing the wall in front of him, Sandro turned around quickly and looked for his wife. Who knows where she was. A man approached him—he had been watching him—placed a hand on his arm, and said, "If I'm not mistaken you are the father!" as he gestured toward Amos, next to the piano. Mr. Bardi nodded, with some embarrassment. "Congratulations! My name is Angelo. I am a hairdresser and I have looked after your son's hair these past few days; I already love him like my best friend."

Amos thanked everyone who had worked so hard for him, he had kind words for the other contestants, less fortunate than he, and sang again the piece to general enthusiasm, before finally posing for the photographers. A good hour passed before he was able to embrace his parents and friends; and only for a few minutes. He had only a moment to grab a bite to eat and was immediately sent to several radio studios to give interview after interview, until five in the morning. There were a few television appearances the next day and finally he could head for home, where he found a truly great surprise.

When he arrived in his father's car near the bridge at Sterza, an enormous banner greeted his return: THANK YOU FOR AN AMAZING PERFORMANCE AT SAN REMO! Beyond the bridge there was a crowd bigger than any he had ever seen before, which stopped the car. The entire town was present to receive and embrace their new hero. Everyone touched him, shook his hand, yelled out greetings, while Sergio, his great friend from childhood, as strong as a Roman wrestler, protected him from the overzealous.

It was a truly moving celebration; impossible to forget; a spontaneous show of affection that only one who has the fortune of living in a small town can understand. Amos, it goes without saying, was infinitely happy; yet he knew full well that in reality, everything was just beginning.

29

FOR SOME TIME AMOS felt sure that he would awaken
from that marvelous dream and find himself again in bed with the
same problems and the apparently insurmountable difficulties that
he had confronted for so long. Many things had quickly changed in
his life. Now everyone talked about him, some claiming a friendship that, to tell the truth, had never really existed; some recounted
anecdotes in which they starred with Amos, which in reality were
only the fruit of their vain imaginations. Amos was always very
amused, often laughing until tears came to his eyes.

Many practical problems, at least those most immediate, had
been swept away by the unexpected turn of events that caused him
to emerge the winner; his private life, though, became more public
property day by day; the veil that had always protected him became
more and more transparent, and this made Amos suffer, as did the
attitude of some of his neighbors and acquaintances, who simply
could not behave in his presence as they had always done before.
Now he felt himself continually under observation, and in certain
ways irrationally praised. Not that there was any insincerity in his
dealings with others; just that the sense of spontaneity that Amos
was accustomed to was gone. At times he felt that something made
him different in the eyes of other people, and to himself he wished

that time would restore things to the way they were before. In addition, the number of commitments that took him far from home grew day by day.

Elena went with him almost everywhere, happy and at the same time worried by this sudden change in their habits. Amos sought to reassure her; he told her that marriage was supposed to give two people a sense of serenity, the greatest gift, which every-one had to defend at all costs.

One night, returning home after a long day in the studio with Carlo, Amos found his wife waiting for him out in the courtyard. It was late June and one could easily stay outside at night, but her agitation seemed strange to him.

Elena seemed particularly happy: she accompanied him into the house arm in arm, and only when the door was closed, with the air of one who cannot find the right words, did she reveal to her husband that she was expecting a child. She was happy, happier than Amos had ever seen her. From the kitchen came a smell that made his mouth water, and there was even a bottle of champagne in the refrigerator to celebrate the extraordinary event. In his way, Amos was happy, but he was happy above all for his wife. He had never had a great passion for babies; surely he would love his own children, but he couldn't imagine how and how much, and he was becoming curious about that experience which he knew changed the lives of everyone. In any event, Elena's joy was contagious and Amos never looked back. She began to involve him in a thousand and one small projects: the layout of the baby's room, the things to buy, the small modifications necessary to make the house safe for the baby.

Amos, in the meantime, was preparing to debut in the role of Macduff in Verdi's *Macbeth*. It was to be staged at the local theater and this filled him with satisfaction; it appeared to him—who knows why?—as a sign of destiny, and above all an authentic chal-lenge to the skeptics who had repeatedly affirmed that it would be absolutely impossible for a blind man to tread the boards of the stage. And the words of Goethe came back to him: "To live in the idea means to consider the impossible as possible." He studied with zeal, and when rehearsals began he made himself well liked thanks to his diligence: he was always the first to arrive and the last to leave, he listened to advice and did everything possible to please the conductor and the director, and not to be a hindrance to his colleagues.

The tickets were selling like hotcakes: an atmosphere of affection and recognition surrounded Amos, who, for obvious reasons, felt emotional and full of responsibility.

Dressed in the heavy wool costume of a warrior, Amos sat in his dressing room and began warming up his voice. A few minutes before the start of the opera, he was already soaked in a cold sweat, despite the fact that it was September and still hot. The theater was filled to capacity. Although his role was no big deal, at that moment it seemed insurmountable. He knew that he had to pay close attention to his colleagues' voices onstage so as not to miss his cue. But he was certain of one thing: in the depths of his soul, Amos could identify completely with a man who in the end manages to triumph over wickedness. It was a role that he loved, and the audience understood that immediately.

When he made his entrance, surrounded by three ballerinas—symbolizing the tragic memory of Macduff's three sons, killed at the hands of a merciless tyrant—he thought of his unborn child and was profoundly moved. His voice was filled with the sadness of a man who has suffered but who has struggled mightily. At the end of the aria, before his voice fell silent, suffocated by emotion, a thundering ovation rose from the theater, thus assuring Amos that his performance had been a success. Until very recently, he had been singing in piano bars, performing before a distracted audience. He thought about this for a moment and a feeling of pure gratitude rose in his heart.

Around the same time, Amos was invited by Pavarotti to participate in a television show, in which they would sing a duet. The call came at night. He had already gone to bed, but when the phone rang, he woke with a start. A voice said, "Good evening, this is Luciano Pavarotti . . ." At first, still half-asleep, Amos thought it was a joke, but then he recognized the unmistakable timbre of the maestro's voice. Only a few years earlier, Amos had tried to approach the maestro to shake his hand and congratulate him, but the security guards wouldn't let him pass. But now he was actually speaking to him. How was it possible? Amos asked himself this question, and in the meantime went ahead, without preoccupying himself with the tiredness and discomfort that the sudden change of attitude, that brusque detachment from things, inevitably provokes.

At the beginning of October he was invited by his record company to Bologna to record a new album. Amos was really worried about the selection of songs. He understood that it was absolutely necessary that at least one song went straight to people's hearts: if that record wasn't a success, all the work done until that point would have been for naught. On the other hand, what could he do? The company had a contract and agreements had to be respected; for him the only thing to do was to record the album, putting his whole heart into it, and hope. But the surprises of that year were not quite finished. Toward the middle of December, he was invited to sing at a concert at the Vatican, in the Nervi Hall. It was such a great honor to perform there, alongside famous artists from all over the world—an enormous recognition. On that occasion, as always, Amos gave his all and the audience that filled the hall received him warmly.

A few days later he and Elena departed for Stockholm, where he was to participate in a year-end concert. It was truly an unforgettable experience. The difficulties began just outside the airport because of a communication problem: Amos understood very little English and it seemed as though his hosts understood only a little as well; they—understandably—knew not a word of Italian. Everything became so difficult, even the simplest things, although everyone was very kind and generous with them. In addition, it was freezing, and Amos was worried for Elena's health. She was now seven months pregnant, with a big belly that never failed to astound him. He thought of Italy, of his friends, reunited to celebrate the end of the year all together, and he felt homesick and alone, as he had never felt before then; on the night of the concert, locked in his dressing room, he wanted to cry; but he was ashamed of his weakness, gathered his strength, and went onstage, even though the expression on his face was one of a condemned man and not one of an up-and-coming artist.

He returned to Italy as happy as a boarding-school student returning for the holidays, and immediately went to work. The San Remo Festival was coming soon; something that Amos both wanted and didn't want. The piece that he had already recorded was undoubtedly interesting, out of the ordinary, but it seemed to him to be too refined, too elegant, and was missing the emotional impact that was necessary in such situations, where everything was on the line for only five minutes. "This song," he said to Michele and Caterina, "is not right for what we want to do."

"But we don't have anything better," they answered him, "and the piece is very beautiful. You must believe in it with all your heart, and defend it with all your strength. Anyway, one can't just stay on the sidelines and watch; one can't miss an opportunity like this."

So Amos resigned himself to the facts. Things had to be this way, and it was useless to try to contradict the flow of events. Better to swim with the tide, taking care to watch out for the rapids. So that's what he did. He left for San Remo in the cold and rain one February morning in a car specially sent to Poggioncino to take him to the city of flowers. Just like a year ago, but this time he left without his family. Elena had decided it would be more prudent to remain at home rather than risk giving birth in a hospital where she knew no one. Amos would have preferred to bring her with him: according to his calculations there was time to go and come back before the happy event, but he raised no objection. He only asked that his wife be careful and make sure she was never alone for any reason; then he left.

The stay in San Remo was, from the beginning, pleasant and less tiring than he'd expected. With him were Adriano; Pier Paolo, a young musician and good friend of Amos's; and his parents. He sang on the night of February 21. He gave it his all, but undoubtedly his concentration was not at his usual level; and the song, he knew very well, wasn't the kind that immediately seizes an audience. In the preliminary voting he wasn't even among the top ten. It was exactly what Amos had feared from the beginning. In first place was a young singer, also managed by Michele. Amos knew full well the consequences of that situation: Michele would surely devote all his energies to the new singer, setting Amos aside. It was terrible. Everything might collapse; he would have to begin from the beginning, to the joy of his detractors, those who in the course of that year had had to bite their tongues for having spoken too soon. How many ugly things might be said about him! With a smile on their lips the detractors would say. "I always said he wouldn't accomplish anything, it was only a stroke of good luck . . ."

All these thoughts whirled in Amos's mind and upset him, while Michele pretty much disappeared from sight. The situation was obviously critical; Amos was defeated, but he had not lost his combative spirit. On the other hand, what could he do now to salvage a situation that was apparently already lost?

He ran to his room and asked not to be disturbed for any reason. He had to rest and clear his mind to regain his serenity. What would Ettore have suggested? Would everything really return to the way it was before? Was the weight of defeat so crushing? Buried in those gloomy thoughts, he slowly fell asleep. Suddenly a noise woke him, then he heard the voice of his mother. "Why have they woken me?" he thought. An expression of annoyance was stamped on his face; he was about to say something rude when he again heard his mother saying "It's a boy, it's a boy! Everything's fine, everything's great!" He sat bolt upright in bed. "Calm down, I told you that everything's fine! Elena is fine. You rest and don't worry about anything. I'm sorry, but I had to tell you right away!" She kissed her son and left the room, closing the door.

Amos couldn't go back to sleep. A flood of thoughts kept him company: a new life had been born, to be raised in his house; and how would that child turn out? It was the first time the thought had crossed his mind. He realized that he absolutely could not wait for the end of the festival to see his child; and he felt a certain remorse for not being at his wife's side during those hours that are so important for a couple. Who knew how much she had suffered and missed him, since she was used to having him always around.

Suddenly he thought of the festival and felt a pang in his heart; his position in the rankings was truly desperate. He was making a bad impression just when he should have honored the birth of his first son with a great performance. A profound sadness enveloped him: woe betide anyone who would tell him that the blessed event was much more important than a victory at the festival . . . ah, how false were those speeches! A father must be an example to his son, he must fight to win: in every enterprise everyone must give their best, thereby setting an example to others. Precisely for this reason he *had* to find the strength to put aside all those useless worries and concentrate his best energies on the task at hand.

Thus, seeking to reassure himself, he prepared for the next night and climbed onto the stage motivated and full of good intentions. Nevertheless he still did not improve his position in the rankings. Amos was seated in a restaurant with his parents when the results of the voting were brought to him. Immediately he lost his appetite and stopped eating. He turned to his father and said, "I absolutely *must* join Elena, I have two free days and I cannot remain here . . ."

Mr. Bardi immediately understood that it would be useless to try to change his son's mind. His wish was legitimate, and he agreed to accompany his son to the hospital in Volterra where

Elena had given birth and where she was to remain for another few days. During the trip, Amos didn't open his mouth. A slight feeling of dread had taken hold of him and he could not fight it. He feared that he would not love his son, that he would remain indifferent to the first physical contact with that child that had just been born, and he was tormented by the idea of the unhappiness it would cause Elena, toward whom he now felt a renewed sense of tenderness and gratitude.

When he reached the small room in which the small crib had been placed between two small beds, he felt his heart beating furiously. He breathed deeply, as he did before going onstage, and entered. He approached Elena's bed and hugged her timidly, afraid of hurting her. Lying in that hospital bed, she suddenly seemed very fragile; he asked how she was feeling and then remembered the child and, forcing himself to feign an interest he didn't in truth yet have, he approached the crib and carefully felt for the newborn. The little boy was sleeping peacefully. The fear of waking him could have provided an excellent pretext for delaying the first contact, but a strange curiosity conquered all his hesitations. He reached out and, with a delicacy that he never imagined he was capable of, picked up his son and placed him against his chest.

A faint and vaguely sweet but unique smell, which Amos immediately recognized as the smell of newborns, rose to his nose and was diffused all around him. Amos breathed it in deeply and for the first time in his life felt as though he were really drunk; he brushed his lips against the cheeks of the baby, and when he decided to say something he realized that he was alone with his wife in that small hospital room. Everyone else had left so as not to disturb the complex mix of sentiments, sensations, and emotions that are the most intimate, the most profound and indestructible forces within any family. In those brief moments Amos understood that a new form of love had put down deep and ineradicable roots in his heart. Everything had happened in a way that was both quick and surprising, and he now felt himself a new person. Suddenly everything fell into place, and he understood those things that are truly important. That seemingly weak and insignificant creature of which he was the father and for whom, without any hesitation, he would have been ready to give his own life, immediately became the most important thing in the world.

The doctor allowed him to remain at Elena's side for the entire night; to Amos it seemed a favor worthy of eternal gratitude. He said good-bye to his father and with the little boy on his chest lay down on the empty bed, promising his wife to gently lay him down in the crib before he fell asleep. But Amos wasn't sleepy and it seemed that the infant was listening to his heart beat. He felt a new emotion, deep and mysterious, which grew with every small movement of the child, with his every cry. Next to him was a woman who had created life itself, and he, Amos, was the father of that creature. This thought seemed to him an enormity, something so complex that it couldn't register in his mind; and yet it was true. Amos thought deeply, and in the meantime he delicately caressed the face of that little angel and that fragile body. He whispered nonsense to him, full of sentiment, until he got the impression that the baby had fallen asleep. Then he remained motionless in bed, afraid that he might disturb the child, and slowly began to put together verses that summarized, in some way, the sensations and thoughts of those unforgettable hours:

Like a giant,
Proud and happy I embrace my little one; the small, tender body, innocent,
Fragile and alive, like a little lost bird I press against my chest
Quiet and sure, half-asleep
For some instant, almost sweetly
My destiny appears as if in a dream. Thus I see myself old and resigned,
Seated there beside the fireplace;
Anxiously awaiting a child
In the evening, to hear him suddenly return with the gift of a smile,
A word, a kindness

And like a promise that consoles
The immense joy of a caress . . .
Then I awake and have already forgotten, but within my enraptured soul
I notice that the newborn child
Is already worth more than my own life.

For several hours Amos forgot the festival, the difficulties of his career, his own future even. An undefinable sense of gratitude toward the whole world, a kind of emotional inebriation, took complete hold of him. He slowly got up from the bed and began walking up and down the room with the child in his arms.

There is one man to whom I owe the little that I know, he thought. A man who has taught me that it is better to do than to speak; that it is better to doubt than have unshakable certainties; that it is more important to be than to have. I will give this child Ettore's name so that I will remember him always, even when he is no longer with us.

Happy with this idea, which he was sure Elena would agree to, he went toward the crib and put the child down; then he lay down on the bed and tried to rest a bit, before the ordeal of the next few days.

3 O

IN THE EARLY HOURS of the morning, Amos left for San Remo. He was sad to leave his wife and child, but his sense of duty called.

On the night of the final he felt in perfect form, and even found the calm necessary to give a good performance. The audience began to recognize and appreciate his piece. The reception was extremely warm and his place in the rankings was much better; yet he could not get past fourth place. For him it was still a burning disappointment, one he must realistically consider as the beginning of an unstoppable decline. But what was he to do? He had to gather his strength and do as he always did. Now there was also a child to raise, a child would look to follow his father's example; therefore it was absolutely necessary that he redouble his efforts.

So, without losing sight of his studies, Amos threw himself into promoting his new record, traveling with Carlo always at his side, throughout Europe, fighting off tiredness and the boredom of the interminable waiting in airports and the waiting rooms of radio and television stations. Elena waited for him at home with the baby and seemed serene, conscious of the importance of all these trips, which nevertheless left her alone and afraid. Then, in October, they departed together for a long tour of Belgium, Holland, Germany, France, and Spain. The show was very original: a great orchestra played symphonic pieces and then accompanied famous singers in all sorts of musical genres. The audiences seemed to enjoy the concert very much and every night the venues were sold out.

Amos's record company had managed to get him on the tour, and amid the general surprise, after the first performances, he began to sell an impressive number of records in those countries. Thus began a period of very difficult work that forced Amos to travel widely for nearly three hundred days of the year, an effort that produced incredible results. In a very brief space of time Amos's albums began to sell out everywhere; in Germany for example, the company that produced the CD had to work over the weekends to satisfy the demand, which to some appeared unprecedented. More or less the same thing happened in France just a few months later and then again in America, where the barrier for those singers who don't speak English appears almost insurmountable.

What was happening? Everyone was asking him this, including Michele, who lost no time and threw himself into Amos's new project, abandoning everything else to concentrate all his energies on the career of the singer, which, day after day, seemed more and more to resemble a marvelous fairy tale. Amos was competing strenuously for the top of the record charts all over the world both in popular music and classical music: on one side the record company called him to promote his records; on the other the most prestigious theaters and concert halls in the world insistently requested his performances, offering him fees that made his head spin, and to which it was difficult to say no, especially for someone like Amos, who was still afraid that he wouldn't even be able to support his family. And yet, despite the atmosphere of euphoria, overwhelming success, and his changed economic situation, Amos tried in some way not to change his lifestyle or above all himself. In his heart he always had his family, his friends, those people who had awaited his return from the festival and who had welcomed him with that immense banner on which was written: THANK YOU FOR AN AMAZING PERFORMANCE AT SAN REMO. He would never forget it.

In every part of the world, his true, frank, and spontaneous Tuscan voice, always humble and respectful but never submissive, was broadcast. Perhaps this was the recipe that made him popular with both the Holy Father as well as the president of the United States, both of whom, after hearing him for the first time, invited him back to perform again. Amos said the same thing to himself that he said to journalists, ironic in a certain sense but also truly religious: "Our path has been willed from above, and one can only do what He has willed."

Time passed quickly and events—each more incredible than the last—followed each other at an almost unsustainable pace. The fact was that because of his changed life and constant commitments, which were ever more pressing, Amos was forced to consider the necessity of moving to a more comfortable place. The acquisition of a new house, the first that was truly his own, also resolved some problems concerning the investment of his first earnings. Therefore, after long and complicated searching, he and Elena decided to buy a beautiful house in the heart of Versilia, near the sea, and with the Apuane Mountains making an incomparable work of natural art as backdrop. There, in addition, he would finally be free from the allergies that had made him suffer so much in his youth.

It was at that time that Elena became pregnant with their second child, another boy, who was named Andrea. This time Amos managed to be by Elena's side for the blessed event, and was once more overjoyed by it, so painful in the waiting, so joyous after the birth. The newspapers competed to spread the news, enriched with the most curious details, some true, some completely invented. Amos wasn't particularly happy about this, but by now he was used to the idea that he no longer possessed any privacy.

It was one of the most beautiful periods in Amos's life, despite his physical and psychological fatigue and some health problems with those dearest to him. He felt that he had the wind in his sails; he gave thanks for being alive, for the immense satisfactions that life gave him and which he dedicated to his parents, who had done so much for him and who had worried so much, suffering in silence, in the fear that he wouldn't realize his dreams.

But there was a problem that continually tormented Amos: the constant conflict with his own voice, which not only refused to bend to his wishes but was different every day. New problems continually arose for which not even the most renowned experts had quick and definitive solutions. And it was also necessary to solve the most thorny and at the same time most important question of the high notes, which Amos felt he had not solved once and for all. "With the beautiful middle range that you have, you can sing well, but it's with the high notes that one makes money!" a famous teacher had told him once, to push him to study more. Amos felt very frustrated: he couldn't possibly continue to sing songs in which there were no really high notes. Soon he would become a target for criticism that could destroy his career. For this reason he thought about his voice day and night with an almost maniacal intensity. At times he would try a high note in the middle of the night, while the entire family was sleeping peacefully. He could never fall asleep with some doubt lingering in his mind about his voice or with a new trick to experiment with. Elena would awaken with a start and would be angry, even though she was aware—knowing her husband well—that reproving him would never stop him. Amos would always beg for forgiveness, sincerely sorry, but he knew that he couldn't promise that it wouldn't happen again, maybe even the very next night.

But with time, practice, and a bit of good luck even the high notes began to come. The first ones were small and trembling, yet he improved day by day with an amazing rapidity, so much so that the high register eventually became his most secure range. Then he had the problem of tying together the various registers; but this type of work was for him much easier than the previous problem. If the road ahead seemed to be an uphill struggle, full of difficulties and obstacles, at least he was beginning to see a little light at the end of the tunnel; light that gave him strength and courage. And Amos knew he could never give up just when his career had taken off after so many false starts.

One day he received an invitation to participate in a concert in Bremen, Germany, to celebrate the one hundredth anniversary of one of the most famous and prestigious record companies in the world, Deutsche Grammaphon. Amos was honored by the invitation and accepted immediately; an arrangement was quickly made on the part of both sides. He telephoned Ettore with the intention of inviting his old friend to accompany him. So much time had passed since he had seen his friend, and he wanted to know his opinion on certain things that had happened recently, about which Amos had not been able to form a clear opinion; from their meeting, Amos would have been able to ascertain how and to what extent success had changed his character, in addition to his lifestyle. In other words, Ettore would surely have encouraged an examination of conscience that Amos wished to undertake to feel more tranquil, more at peace with himself.

For deep down, Amos wasn't happy. All that money, which forced him to change his ways; the clashes—sometimes harsh—with his collaborators, agents, record-company executives; the attacks in the press, by critics, all this was extremely tiring and hurtful. He wanted to speak to his old friend, who, he was sure, would be a great help.

Ettore immediately accepted the invitation. He loved to travel, and besides it had been some time since he had seen Amos in person rather than on a TV screen. He arrived at the airport, punctual as always, dressed as usual in jeans, sweater, and sneakers. As agile and fit as a man in his prime, Ettore carried his sixty-six years incredibly well; yet Amos noted in him a slight change that disturbed him somewhat. It seemed that in certain moments Ettore was absent, distracted, as if his mind was elsewhere. Amos, worried, thought for the first time about Ettore's age: he wondered how that man—so sure, unassailable, as healthy and strong as an oak—would handle illness or doctors (he who had never once in his life been ill or turned to doctors), or a slow decline in a hospital. Was Ettore also thinking of this? Was he also searching for a solution to the problem, he who always had a solution for the problems of others? Amos tried to dispel the thought; there was a magnificent sunset and it was quite warm, and this put him in a good mood.

During the trip, Ettore returned to his old self, prolific with advice: he did not spare his young friend some paternal reproofs, for which Amos was sincerely grateful. On the plane a flight attendant touched Amos's shoulder, getting his attention: "Sorry, Mr. Bardi, may I have your autograph?" she asked in English. He folded out the small table and took a piece of paper and pen from the hand of the young woman and wrote "Cordially yours" above his signature. The woman, smiling, put the paper and pen back in her pocket and then took his hand between hers and shook it warmly: "Oh, it's very kind of you! Do you know, all my family loves you!"

"Thank you, it has been a pleasure for me!" Amos replied in English to the woman, who had still not let go of his hand.

Ettore, in the meantime, had opened his newspaper. When the flight attendant left, he turned and said jokingly to Amos: "Hey, Count Vronsky, you think she was Anna Karenina? Remember," he added in English, "you have a family with two children."

"What are you saying?" Amos quickly parried in English.

"Nothing, nothing . . . only I know you too well!" answered Ettore, still in English. In fact, Ettore had been the one to give Amos his first smattering of English and now he was pleased to see his progress.

"Don't worry," concluded Amos, laughing.

In Bremen, Ettore attended one of Amos's concerts for the

first time, and when it was over he ran to warmly shake his hand, congratulating him. Who knows what Amos would have given to know exactly what his friend, seated in the audience among the public, was thinking, seeing him climb onto the stage beside the famous conductor and perform before all these people who knew and loved and lived music and who could make so many comparisons and severe judgments ... Who knows if Ettore once again had found the time to observe all those faces and analyze the scene with his usual intelligence and insight, or whether he had abandoned himself for the first time to just listening, really moved? Amos would never know.

31

❧❧❧

ON THE DAY OF HIS fortieth birthday, Amos, surrounded by all his dearest friends, had much to celebrate and be happy about: in just a few years he had attained incredible goals, goals he had never dared hoped for. He was at the top of the charts in both classical and pop music, he had dozens of platinum records, prizes and recognition everywhere, theaters and concert halls competing to attract him, to the joy and amazement of Michele, who could not believe his eyes at the offers that arrived at his office from every part of the world.

Amos, in spite of everything, had remained the boy he always was and loved to share his happiness with his friends: Adriano, Verano, Carlo, Luca, Giuliano, the old Monti (that's what he liked to call the man who needed to hear only a few notes to fall in love with his voice and at his own risk had created false papers to have Amos make his professional debut at the Valli Theater in Reggio Emilia) . . . There was even Sergio, a tennis pro Amos had befriended lately, because they shared a way of seeing the world, and with whom a friendship had been born as precious and as transparent as Bohemian crystal.

All his friends had accepted Amos's invitation, and the birthday party was among the happiest that he had ever had. The banquet had been organized by Verano, and Mr. Bardi had brought a lot of excellent wine: no one that night, it seemed, was worried about their health! The jokes, songs, and pleasant stories lasted until past two o'clock when tiredness began to creep in, and the first guests went home.

Before his father left, Amos went to him and said, "My cousin Giovanni has invited me so many times to go out with him on his boat and I've never had the opportunity to do so; tomorrow morning I'm free and the weather is promising: what do you say to a sea trip?"

"Call me tomorrow around nine and I'll tell you," said his father, giving a quick glance at his watch. Then he left, too.

❧

As soon as the alarm clock rang, Amos jumped out of bed and dressed quickly. Elena followed him, although she was very tired, and went to the kitchen to prepare some milk for the children. Ettore was sleeping so soundly in his parents' big bed that no noise could possibly disturb him. Amos, meanwhile, anxiously awaited the hour agreed upon to call his parents and go out with them in his cousin's boat. When it was almost time, a few minutes before nine, he dialed the number and waited. No one answered; why? After five or six rings he recognized his mother's voice and knew immediately that something was wrong.

"So," he asked, "are you ready, or are you still lolling about in bed?" There was a pause. Then Mrs. Bardi sighed and in an uncertain tone of voice said: "Amos, I don't think you'll want to go out on the boat today." "Why?" asked Amos, with a sinking feeling. He knew his mother well, and from her tone of voice he had guessed her state of mind. Her tone frightened him, so much so that for a few brief, terrible moments he thought about his loved ones. What could have happened and to whom? The children were there with him under his vigilant protection, and Elena was in the kitchen.

He thought of his father, his little brother, but his mother interrupted his thoughts and said: "Yesterday afternoon Ettore fell from his bicycle and hit his head on the pavement." Then she stopped; she couldn't find the right words. Amos felt his face become hot, while a sudden weakness in his legs forced him to sit down on the edge of the bed, next to his son, who was slowly waking up. "What happened?" asked Amos, practically yelling into the telephone. "Amos . . . I'm so sorry . . . It didn't end well . . ." said his mother, knowing the pain her son must be feeling. For several moments they remained silent. Amos was stunned; it seemed as if the world was spinning around him and he was completely bewildered. All of a sudden, with a sickening clarity, everything became clear. Ettore was dead; he would never see him again, never hear his voice again. Passing from this life, Ettore could no longer advise him, push him, comfort him. Their friendship was finished forever . . .

Without uttering a word, with an hysterical gesture, Amos slammed down the receiver. He jumped to his feet and like a madman, he ran to the stairs yelling, "Elena! Elena! Ettore is dead! Elena! Elena . . ." She, meanwhile, was pouring the hot milk into cups decorated by her children. When she heard her husband's voice she put down the pan, trying to understand what he was saying so hysterically. Suddenly the meaning of Amos's cries struck her, hard. She felt a terrible pang in her heart and a lacerating pain in her stomach, her eyes filled with tears, and a desperation that she had never felt until then seized her so violently that she almost fell. Yet she recovered her strength and ran up the stairs like a robot; she crossed the hallway, entered the bedroom, and racked with sobs, threw herself onto the bed next to little Ettore, who watched her in wide-eyed terror. "Ettore! Ettore!" cried the poor mother pathetically; only little by little did she begin to realize that her son was alive and well. She embraced him with all her strength, like a madwoman. She pressed him to her breast, and looked at her husband. Amos had covered his face with his hands and was on his knees on the carpet next to the bed. "Do you want to kill me? I thought I was going to die!" she yelled to him between the tears that appeared to suffocate her.

"Why are you crying, Mamma?" asked Ettore in a small voice, visibly upset. "Who's dead? What was Daddy saying before?" Amos got up and went to the child, who had freed himself from his mother's embrace and sat himself on the pillow, observing his parents with confusion.

Poor Amos took the child in his arms and began to speak to him tenderly, in a low voice: "Do you remember Ettore? That good man who had your name? He is no more."

"What do you mean, Father, he's no more?" asked Ettore, who was at that stage when children ask the reasons for everything.

"No! I made a mistake," continued Amos, overcome by emotion. "He is and will always be, but we won't be able to see him; but we can still remember him and carry him in our hearts. Okay?" "Okay, Father," answered the small boy, and quickly ran off.

Amos shut himself in his study, sat down at the desk, and began to think: the death of Ettore seemed absolutely inconceivable. How could such a stupid accident have ended the life of such a strong and sure man? Amos had never really given a thought to the possibility that Ettore might die. For him, Ettore was invincible, perfect, as eternal as an idea. But now he was gone, after doing everything that he wanted to do. On his last trip with Amos to Bremen, perhaps he told Amos the last things that needed to be told: a kind of moral testament that Amos would never forget.

32

AMOS ARRIVED AT THE PIAZZA of the church with his soul adrift, filled with a desperation that became, minute by minute, increasingly unbearable. He clenched his fists, took a deep breath, and gathered all his strength so as not to burst into sobs. Elena was walking by his side in silence, not looking up at him. He was aware of his little brother on his other side; behind them were Adriano, Verano, Carlo, Giuliano, in short all his old friends, those who would never abandon him, especially at one of life's most difficult moments.

When Amos entered the church of Lajatico, the church that held so many joys and sweet memories, it was already full of people, all gathered to pay their last respects to Ettore. The coffin was already there, at the foot of the altar, and within it rested a body. A cold shiver of horror passed through Amos and a wave of despair filled his heart. The heat, the penetrating odor of incense and flowers, the atmosphere of pain and sorrow affected him to the point that he almost fainted. Elena found him a free place in a pew, and they sat down.

The funeral began, but Amos couldn't pay attention. With his head bowed and his face in his hands, he gave his thoughts free rein, recalling memories both ancient and more recent, and came to only when the priest began to speak of the deceased; then Amos sat up and listened carefully. The parish priest spoke of Ettore's life, of his Christian journey, but everything that he said was so distant, so devoid of real life and truth that it seemed almost offensive to Amos. What is he saying? Who exactly is the priest talking about? Amos began asking himself. Is he really talking about Ettore? Did he know him so little? Or is it that he isn't able to forgive him because he didn't see him regularly enough at Mass? Amos's heart was filled with an unrestrainable indignation and he began pondering the possibility of delivering the eulogy himself before the funeral was finished so that he could bid farewell to Ettore with the proper emotion and affection, saying the things that had to be said, in the way they had to be said. I will speak from the foot of the altar, he thought, next to the coffin, next to him; and I will speak of him to all these people who loved him like me, who like me have received something from him that they cannot forget: a piece of advice, some assistance, a good word. Again he stopped listening and once again lost himself in his thoughts, which were now focused on the speech that he wanted to make. "Dear friends," he would begin, "I hope that you will forgive my need to speak to you briefly about the man whom we all wish to recognize, today more than ever, with love and gratitude. The religious aspects of this ceremony have been covered by our priest; I, as a layperson, feel instead the need to attempt a profile of the extraordinary human, moral, and intellectual qualities of this man so that no one forgets and that nothing, but nothing, of him is truly lost. Today, in this church, conquered by an emotion that fills our eyes with tears and breaks our voices, we bid farewell to a man who departs for a long voyage; but is there any reason to cry for a dead man that departs? Those who have walked by Ettore's side on the path of truth, of humility, of goodwill, of one's daily commitment to one's neighbor, so close to the teachings of Christ the Redeemer, of the Risen Christ, cannot and *should* not think of Ettore as a man who has left us forever, but as a companion who continues to walk by our side and to comfort us with the clarity of his ideas, with those good words that he always had for everyone. Am I perhaps being blasphemous if I ask you to rebel, to rise up in arms against the idea of this death? So be it! I implore you, I beg you to forget this fatal day, when the remains of our brother are enclosed in the shelter of a tombstone and an epigraph. Forget this day and remember *him,* continue to make him live among you; in your houses, in your conversations, as surely you will already have done a thousand other times, when Ettore was far away, on one of his numerous trips to every part of the world. After all, what has really happened? Something has broken, something broke in Ettore, his body has fallen; so what? These are things that happen, but hair and nails fall, too; in forty years every human body is transformed and becomes something completely different, unrecognizable. And does one perhaps despair because of this? No! Certainly not! So why despair so much today if in substance nothing has happened? Everything in this world perishes, even the body! It is no more worthy than beauty, which, as one famous poet says, is like the 'shadow of a flower.' It is not worth more than power, which is like 'a trumpet's echo that is lost in the valley.' No! The only thing that is important is that the *idea of what was* remains intact, that part of him that is in us is preserved. Because the idea and *only* the idea 'wins over fleeing time and barbarous silence' . . ."

Amos's heart was filled with the courage that makes men launch themselves into the fray of battle, disdainful of the tremendous risk that awaits them. That sudden idea of speaking to the assembled faithful and of somehow removing Ettore from the embrace of death and consigning him forever to the memory of those who loved him gave him a bracing calmness.

He was about to get up to go toward the altar when he heard a song that suddenly shook him from his reverie: it was the sad, solemn song with which the dearly departed are accompanied on their final voyage. The coffin, carried by four young men from the town, passed before him just at that moment, and the people were leaving the pews and beginning to follow the procession.

Amos's eyes filled with tears, big hot tears that streaked down his face. His sobs shook his chest. He had said nothing of what he had wanted to say, or rather cry out, and now it was too late. He slipped into the crowd like an outsider, and slowly followed the procession to the small graveyard, a few hundred yards from the town, shaded by the dark green cypresses of his beautiful Tuscany.

EPILOGUE

A FEW DAYS LATER Amos departed for the United States for a series of concerts. With him were Carlo, Michele, and Cristina, his secretary, whom Amos admired for her patience and the effort she put into her work. The Americans loved Amos fanatically and welcomed him with open arms. The tickets for his concerts were sold out everywhere from the very first day that they went on sale . . .

Amos's story, though, ends here. Everything that followed is by now in the public domain, because of all the attention the media have devoted to his story from the beginning. It is better to end with some passages from his diary so as to leave Amos to conclude his own story in his own words:

1 October 1998

I depart with death in my heart, but I depart, all the same, full of life and hope. I depart alone, without my family, a loss that makes me suffer much. But I carry Ettore with me, among the people that I will meet, the people that I will speak to or simply shake hands with, and that will be a great comfort . . .

5 October 1998

The American people seem to love me. At my concerts, the public is fantastic, and there simply aren't the words to describe the warmth that welcomes and sustains me. If only every one of them knew the fear with which I get onstage, if they only knew my anguish, my silences, my loneliness ...

7 October 1998

I sometimes have the very unpleasant impression of having become a moneymaking machine and of being treated accordingly. I have become the center of great and competing interests. I am afraid, and I am ashamed of being afraid, because a man who gives his best should never be afraid of anything, even of making a mistake ...

9 October 1998

I have discovered that I am the innocent cause of a struggle between two powerful organizations and have become caught in their crossfire, but a saint must be helping me, or maybe helping me to retreat in an orderly fashion; anyway, I have already been very fortunate: I have enough to live, and above all, I know how to live with little.

12 October 1998

Today I was very moved: arriving in Boston, I found an enormous crowd waiting for me at the airport and discovered that the authorities had proclaimed today Bardi's Day, a holiday in occasion of my concert; but to what can I ascribe such benevolence?

15 October 1998

I still can't believe it: this morning I met the mayor of New York, who gave me a big crystal apple, the symbol of the city. He is a sincere fan of opera and in his speech praised the quality of my voice. Then it was my turn to speak, and in my lame English I said, "I have always been convinced that life is truly a marvelous mystery. This meeting with you today, Mr. Mayor, like my meeting with so many people who live in this country, has only confirmed this idea. As an Italian, I have promised myself to be worthy of this honor, honoring my country and all those who had to leave it."

In any event, in all honesty, I really cannot explain to myself the reason for all this fuss. Perhaps one day, who knows, I may decide to write a book about my life, to satisfy the curiosity of my children and my grandchildren, and to pass the time which in the dressing rooms of theaters and television studios passes so slowly; or to discover, after the fact, what arcane secret has guided a blind child, born and raised in the remote countryside, toward goals so ambitious as to surpass the confines of any fervent imagination.

20 October 1998

Tonight, too, I must sing; therefore I must remain all day here, shut up in this anonymous hotel room, without exchanging a word with anyone, to ensure that my voice conserves all its harmonies; but all in all it's better this way because I am tired. Tired of traveling constantly, tired of ratings, of struggles, of contracts, tired of newspapers that say whatever they want about me, without thinking of the trouble they can do to me, tired of the critics who turn their spiteful artillery fire against my success. Clinging to their princes, forgetting that no one is the repository of absolute truths, they ignore the facts; but princes fall while the facts remain. That's how I think of my fate, and no one can imagine how dear to me, in the solitude of this room, is the music of silence.

AUTHOR'S NOTE

TO THE PATIENT READER who has arrived here, some clarification is owed. You have surely understood that the principal aim of this book consists of the desire to capture at least approximately myself, my conception of life, and above all my conscience today, rather than talk about the world of show business seen from behind the curtains, from dressing rooms, from the halls of television and radio studios.

I have given myself a different name and have done the same for certain others in these memories so as to recount some episodes with the most rigorous historical truth, on the one hand, and on the other, to respect the personality and above all the private lives of those who have been included without expressing a desire to be so. Thus I have been able to recount sins without revealing the sinner. For some famous people, however, I have left their own names with the certainty that they will have nothing to reproach me with.

Now there is nothing left to do but take my leave with pardons, thanks, gratitude, and the hope—allow me this small sin of vanity—of having wrung some boredom and idleness from your time.

Andrea Bocelli

ENDNOTE

Dear Parents and Elena,

I hope you will receive this odd composition that I dedicate to you with all my heart with love, as a profound testament of recognition for the affection and understanding that you have always bestowed upon me, and for the faith that you have placed in me. In these pages, you will easily recognize episodes and aspects of your life that I have decided to describe. I wanted this story to be rooted in truth, if only partially, because it is my own, and even it springs from a mind that has tried to the utmost to clear the field of prejudices and preconceptions that would have compromised the little bit of good that one can find here. And, just as it is dedicated to you, so is it dedicated to my little children, the primary reason for my existence.

How many attempts have I made to understand the world, the society in which we live—so complex and contradictory—and to discover some magic formula, some miraculous prescription, to pass onto my children in order to protect them against the difficulties and challenges of life, which are so frequent and so inevitable. Yet nothing, *nothing* comes to me! Nothing absolutely certain, absolutely good and just! Nothing except for some brief considerations, some innocuous reflections, from which some elementary convictions spring that have allowed me to live a serene and tranquil life, dedicated to the pursuit of an inner peace that only rarely has abandoned me.

What better occasion could I have found than this to offer my children the advice, which springs spontaneously from the depths of my heart, never to lose the capacity to look toward the future with optimism, to cultivate faith in themselves and, above all, faith in their neighbors, upon whom, more than anything else, they will depend? My children will read these pages when they are older and they will see me perhaps as a nostalgic old man, incapable of understanding their problems, closed within a shell of memories, and as irrelevant as a losing lottery ticket.

Here, then, is the reason for this book, in which I have endeavored to recount the joy and luck of a man who in the course of his life has learned to struggle long and hard, with the hope of embracing his own ideals, without, however, believing himself to be the repository of absolute truth, and with doubt always close at hand.

With the passage of time, I have learned to think before I act, and to weigh matters, according to my conscience, before believing something or making a judgment. This has been a hard lesson, and so often my convictions have collapsed, one after another, leaving behind a gnawing doubt. But doubt is the vestal virgin dedicated to the sacred fire of human intelligence; therefore, I accept it, despite the fact that its logical consequence implies that I must discount the very ideas I once believed in and expounded upon.

Human intelligence—like the tremulous flame of a candle in utter darkness—illuminates a very brief stretch of our path ahead, and all around us looms the unknown. Therefore, man advances slowly and cautiously in the direction of the light, choosing only the spot to place his foot, an exercise that convinces him that he is master of his fate.

Looking carefully where one places one's foot and deciding on the right course are always useful endeavors, even if sometimes the path appears sure, but they are still not enough to influence one's destiny significantly. For each of us moves in a direction that is determined from birth. Each moves in that direction with his or her first, uncertain steps and, with a candle, seeks to make a way, to overcome obstacles, often walking more quickly than is prudent.

I believe that humanity, considered as a whole, appears as an immense, disordered procession that advances chaotically, dispelling the darkness with the illumination of innumerable small lights, seeking a goal that is as distant as it is unknown, as sought after as it is incomprehensible. Human life, and the destiny of each one of us, sails on the frailest of boats, riding the currents of a river or a stream that leads finally to the vast sea. In the stern, with rudder in hand, we all seek to avoid collisions or shipwreck but can do nothing to turn back or to stop for a moment of rest.

If the inescapability of events that marks the fundamental nature of humanity constitutes, for me, a profound and deeply rooted conviction, thanks to the illuminating reading of great masterpieces of literature and philosophy, I also know that small, insignificant episodes in the course of my life have made me reflect so much that I have felt the necessity of recounting them so that others may meditate on them and perhaps extract from them something useful.

The destiny of humanity, as well as that of each individual, is, as I see it, predetermined; it is a path guided by an intelligent will which, no matter how one wishes to consider, imagine, idealize, love, hate, beseech, or damn it, can never be rationally understood, simplistically reduced, or attributed to the concept of chance and thereby be ignored.

The drops of rain fall, it is true, according to the designs of chance, descending from the sky to the earth to moisten the roofs of the houses, the leaves of the trees, the streets and the fields; just as the snowflakes, each different from all the others, fall upon the soil, governed by the law of random order, forming an immaculate blanket, which remains on the ground until the rays of the sun melt it away, forever canceling any trace. But the drops of rain, the snowflakes, and the rays of sun themselves are not fruits of chance or of some abstract concept behind which man often hides, confused, resolving in this way what he cannot explain by rules and the laws he knows. When he does so, he commits an act of intellectual presumption, falling precisely where it would be easy to remain standing, with his face illuminated by the smile of the humble who cross the street to avoid the tree of knowledge. Because for the humble, that tree of knowledge holds no interest whatsoever, committed as they are to the effort to remake this earth into that terrestrial paradise from which man was once expelled precisely because of his pride.

TRANSLATOR'S NOTE

TRANSLATING ANDREA BOCELLI'S autobiography has been a great pleasure and honor. That pleasure, though, was tempered by trepidation. Besides the intriguing and delightful voice of Bocelli himself, I found myself accompanied by another voice, always quiet, yet insistent, reminding me of an Italian aphorism: *Traduttore e a traditore* ("The translator is a traitor").

Translating demands a degree of perceptiveness and insight, which hopefully is reflected in this text. There are many words, of course, that lose their nuances and shadings through translation, and there are some words that defy translation at all. The translator wrestles with definitions, sentence structure, grammar, and syntax but must strive to be faithful to the music of the language. Melody is the translator's first concern, but harmony is equally important. Bocelli's polyphonic writing is in various keys: doubt and confidence; fear and awe; reverence and curiosity; determination and self-criticism. One finds herein some profound reflections on music, life, and love, and it is my sincere wish that I have not betrayed the original.